Black Heart

Black Heart

The History of Ley's Malleable
Castings in Derby

–oOo–

The Family and the Foundry

by Bob Read

DB
PUBLISHING

First published in Great Britain in 2005 by

The Breedon Books Publishing Company Limited

Breedon House, 3 The Parker Centre, Derby, DE21 4SZ.

This edition published in Great Britain in 2012 by The Derby
Books Publishing Company Limited, 3 The Parker Centre, Derby,
DE21 4SZ.

ISBN 978-1-78091-191-5

Printed and bound by Copytech (UK) Limited, Peterborough.

Contents

Foreword

I T IS now 17 years since Ley's Malleable Castings ceased trading, and 21 years since I reluctantly and regretfully relinquished my contacts with the company. As the great-grandson of the founder it fell to me, during my term of office, to witness such profound changes to the industrial scene within which we operated, that despite the considerable efforts by all who worked at Ley's and the loyalty that accompanied those efforts, it proved impossible to sustain a viable business.

With the recent demolition of the Baseball Ground, with its many historical connections with Ley's and in particular with my great-grandfather, one of the last remaining features linking us with the history of this area of Derby has gone. Little now remains to remind us of what took place here since Sir Francis purchased his four acres of open land back in 1873.

It is gratifying, however, to see that the land formerly occupied by one of the largest foundries in Europe has been put to good use by the many companies that have sprung up in a location that is now known as the Sir Francis Ley Industrial Park in recognition of my great-grandfather.

Although this area will, hopefully, bear the name of my great-grandfather for a very long time, it is debatable whether the events that occurred here between 1873 and 1987 would be as readily remembered. It is, therefore, very pleasing for me to be associated with the documenting of the events that took place over the 113 years during which Ley's contributed to the rich industrial history of Derby.

Ian Ley
Fauld, 2004

Acknowledgements

PUTTING together the history of Ley's has occupied, albeit on a part-time basis, some three years of research. During the last few years of Ley's existence its archives were either lost or became disseminated and it has taken many hours of searching libraries, record offices and newspaper records to gather the information necessary to be able to piece together the story. During these searches many facts came to light that, although connected with the subject, were peripheral, and perhaps the job would have been completed earlier had I not been tempted to pursue these tangential matters merely out of personal interest. The most enjoyable part of the research was re-establishing contact with many of my ex-colleagues. From these sources came a wealth of information and even though in some cases their contribution may, to them, have seemed of an incidental nature, in many instances it provided a vital link to either complete or confirm a particular issue. I thank all those who contributed in this way and, in particular, for the opportunity to spend a few delightful hours knee-deep in nostalgia.

There are many people I wish to thank for their help and I will attempt to record them below. Not least is a special thank you to my wife, Barbara, for her forbearance and support. Thanks also are due to my daughter-in-law, Helen Meynell, who did the proof-reading and applied her journalistic skills to oversee my grammar.

As I have attempted to relate a story rather than produce a treatise on industrial technology it was essential to link the fortunes of the company to those of the family who for four generations were at the helm. For some of the material necessary to make this connection I am indebted to Sir Ian Ley and Lady Ley, who made me welcome at their home and who so willingly supplied personal information without which the story would be incomplete.

Three years ago I had cause to visit the home of Maxwell Craven when I offered some information regarding Steve Bloomer and his connections with Ley's. During the course of that visit Mr Craven made the remark that with the amount of Ley's material that I had amassed there must be a worthwhile story to tell. As I had been nursing the idea for some time before my encounter with Maxwell Craven, it was undoubtedly his remark on that day that gave me the nudge necessary to embark on the project. For this I thank him and hope that the result of his encouraging comment of three years ago meets with his approval.

The assistance given by the staff at the Derby Local Studies Library and the County Record Offices at Matlock and Nottingham was invaluable. Their knowledge, expertise and friendly willingness to help was always of the highest order on every occasion I called upon their services. This also applies to the archive department of the *Derby Evening Telegraph* together with my gratitude for giving their permission to reproduce some of the photographs herein.

Finally, my thanks are due to the many ex-employees of Ley's and Ewart's, and current employees of Ewart's, with whom I have had the pleasure of renewing acquaintances and who have all made their contribution in adding to the fund of information. These include Paul Atkinson, Mick Baines, Colin Beniston, Ted Goodwin, George and Barbara Gray, the late Jack Hill, Brian Holtham, Keith and Beryl Jones, the late Dennis Parker, Brian Rhodes, Arthur Robins, Ernie Rouse, Dennis Saxelby, Ken Tipping, Nellie Tucker, Keith Tyler, Roger Whitehouse, Ken Williamson, Barry Willison and the Winnals family.

Bob Read
Aston on Trent, Derby

Preface

WALKING around the Colombo Street area of Derby nowadays one would detect little evidence to indicate that only a couple of decades ago there existed a company which, at one stage in its history, was the largest of its kind in Europe.

Ley's Malleable Castings had its headquarters on Colombo Street and conducted its business from a 40-acre site that extended from Osmaston Road for a distance of almost three-quarters of a mile through to Balfour Road in Normanton. Other than Ewart Chainbelt Limited, whose continuing presence on part of the original site is testimony to one of the products on which Ley's laid the basis of their early business success, little else remains to remind us of this once vibrant foundry that flourished for 113 years and provided employment for many thousands of Derby citizens.

The site now accommodates many small and medium-sized businesses on what is known as the Sir Francis Ley Industrial Park. A few forlorn buildings still remain to serve as reminders of a celebrated past, the most notable being the 1904 Messroom in which so many memorable events took place. A little further along Colombo Street stands Ley's Main Office, an elegant building erected in 1925 and formerly a familiar sight to football fans making their way to the Baseball Ground at the end of the street. The Baseball Ground, spiritual home of Derby County Football Club, has recently disappeared from the local landscape and with it has gone yet another tangible link with the history of Ley's. In years to come the remaining buildings will no doubt succumb to the ravages of time, but before these last monuments to a once renowned Derby engineering company leave the scene forever, and memories fade further, it is of historical importance to record the events and human accomplishments associated with this site between 1873 and 1987.

Ley's Malleable Castings was always regarded as a family firm both by the Ley family themselves and by the men and women on the shop floor and in the offices, all of whom felt bound up in the enterprise. It was an enterprise created by a man with energy and entrepreneurial flair, coupled with a compelling will to succeed. Succeed he did and was followed by a further three generations of his family, each of whom in turn nurtured and developed the business principles and codes of conduct laid down by the founder.

There was what might be termed a harsh reality to working at Ley's: the noise, the dirt, the smells and, not least of all, the presence of molten iron and heavy machinery and the dangers they held for the careless or unwary. The shop floor was not a place for the faint-hearted, but perhaps exposure to the arduous and sometimes hazardous conditions, endemic to this type of industry, went some way towards establishing the workplace bonds and company culture. These were just two of the elements which helped to give rise to an extraordinarily high number of employees with long service. In the following narrative there will be numerous examples illustrating the special relationships that existed between workforce and management. These relationships played their part in the breeding of a company culture, the like of which is rarely experienced today.

The rapid development of engineering technology in Victorian Britain, and the resulting expansion of industry in its wake, brought about a migration of population to the areas in which this development was taking place. Derby was no exception, as is borne out by the so-called red brick explosion that occurred in the township of Litchurch during mid to late Victorian times. Originally attracted by employment offered by a number of railway companies, which had established Derby as their centre of operations, this rapidly expanding population not only provided a source of labour but also created a market for goods being manufactured by local factories. During this period, cast iron in its various forms was the available and affordable material to take advantage of the demands of this industrial and domestic expansion, and this is clearly illustrated by the range of products manufactured by Ley's in its early days. Such a situation enabled many companies to put down roots based on this voracious market, and the corporate wealth that it created, but in later years they would become focused on more specialised engineering products.

Francis Ley, the founder of the company, was born, educated and worked in an era which possessed more clearly defined social patterns than the one in which we live today. The relationships that existed between the various levels of society were, generally, to be seen repeated within the workplace, where patronage of the workforce was regarded as a normal and acceptable responsibility of the 'ruling classes'. Patronage in the form of support and encouragement of employees was a prominent feature of life at Ley's over many decades, and the pages that follow will give evidence of the many ways in which those who governed the company gave their time, effort, encouragement and financial support in this direction. Succeeding generations of the Ley family established and gave their support to many welfare activities ranging through sport, health care, and, in the early days, even the setting up of a local chapel to cater for the spiritual needs of the employees and their families.

Some items of historical significance contained in this narrative, for instance newspaper reports, are reproduced as originally printed. No apology is made for this as the events depicted and the style of prose adopted give a valuable insight into the industrial and social cultures of the time.

The story that follows is not an attempt at a definitive industrial history, it is more a celebration of the life and times of a Derby foundry which played such a significant role in the lives of many Derby people past and present.

It is also hoped that it will be accepted as a mark of respect, firstly to the Ley family, who steered the company through more than 100 years of business, and secondly to the generations of Derby men and women who contributed towards placing Ley's Malleable Castings in its significant and justifiable position in Derby's industrial history.

Sir Francis Ley in
1878, age 32.

CHAPTER I

1846 to 1873
The Founder

THE LEY family derive from Mayfield, a few miles from Ashbourne on the Staffordshire side of the River Dove, where, through farming and land ownership going back to the middle of the 16th century, they established themselves among the leading families of the area. The Leys remained at Mayfield for about 200 years until their estate passed out of the senior male line in 1766 when, by marriage, it went to the Greaves of Ingleby. Before this date, however, George Ley, a younger brother of Christopher of Mayfield and grandson of Aden, settled in the Burton on Trent area, and it is from this branch of the family that the founder of Ley's Malleable Castings is descended.

Winshill, on the east side of Burton on Trent, was the home of George Phillips Ley and his wife Sarah, the daughter of a Yoxall farmer, and to them on 3 January 1846 was born their only son Francis. George Phillips Ley, who for over 40 years was the High Bailiff of Burton on Trent County Court, sent his son Francis to the local grammar school. On completion of his education there he was despatched to Whitby in Yorkshire where he received a few years private tutorage. On leaving Whitby, Francis spent several terms at the Royal Agricultural College at Cirencester, the intention being that, in view of his delicate health, he should train to become a gentleman farmer. What was not anticipated, however, was that engineering was to become his natural inclination. His enthusiasm for all things mechanical was presumably so strongly driven that his father had no misgivings in seeing him begin an apprenticeship at Handysides of Derby at the age of 18.

Handysides was a company renowned for producing quality castings for a wide range of engineering, constructional and ornamental purposes. Starting life in 1818 as the Britannia Foundry built by Weatherhead & Glover, it had earned itself a reputation for excellence even before Andrew Handyside took over the firm in 1848. By the time Francis Ley began work there in 1864, carrying with him a recommendation from Mr Michael Thomas Bass, an MP for Derby and a member of the brewing family, Handyside had developed the company even further, such that the opportunities available to learn the skills of iron founding must have been among the finest to be found in the industry.

A profile of Sir Francis Ley published in 1908 gives a clear indication of the enthusiasm and commitment of this new recruit to the Handyside staff. The following extract is from that profile:

> The story is told of a youth of 18, that he frequently worked into the small hours of the morning when there was any important work to be done. One night, about midnight, the manager, on going the rounds of the works, was attracted by a light in the drawing office. Here he found the youth working at the picture drawing of an engine, in order to make sure of it being finished, as it had to go away the next day. 'Humph!' said the manager, on hearing the youth's explanation, 'more than any of the others would have done'. The same incident happened again, but this time the youth was helping one of the men (on a piecework job) who had shown him kindness in connection with the details of engine practice, setting of valves, etc. This time the manager laughed when the youth told him why he was doing the work, but it was a sympathetic laugh, for after that he took an extra kind interest in him, and in six years the latter became a partner in the firm.
>
> That manager was Mr Scott, and that youth, who has since exemplified so brilliantly the poet's words, 'The child is father of

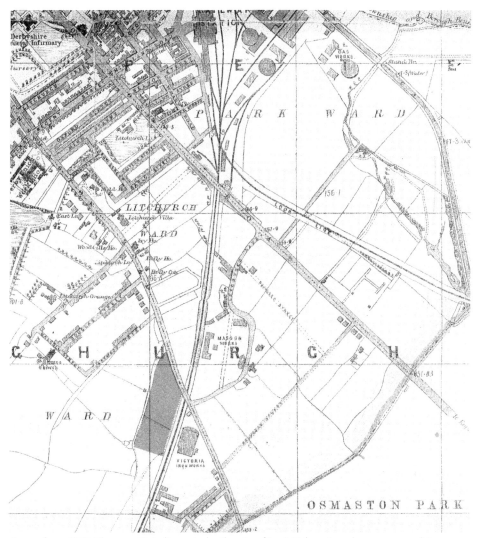

A map from 1867. The area (tinted) was to be the site of Ley's Vulcan Foundry seven years later.

the man,' was none other than Francis Ley, destined to become the head of one of the greatest engineering works in the Midland Counties.

During the ensuing six years, Francis Ley devoted himself to the study of engineering and, in particular, to the many aspects of ironfounding, and at the early age of 24 he became a partner in the firm of Handysides. Also around this time, in August 1870, he was married to Georgina Townsend Willis, daughter of George Willis of Aislaby Hall, near Whitby, North Yorkshire.

A form of malleable iron had been around for some years, but the so-called European method for producing this material was somewhat unreliable and castings were of doubtful quality. In America, the development of malleable iron had moved on at a much faster pace and Francis Ley must have been aware of this. Equally, he must have been conscious of the potential demand for a more ductile iron with which to keep abreast of the ever increasing requirement from the engineering industry for irons of improved performance. He persistently urged the management of Handysides to enter the malleable iron market, but it seems that his colleagues did not share either his enthusiasm or vision, and they did not adopt his proposals. Some three years later, in 1873, Handysides became a limited company and Francis Ley retired from its management in favour of Alexander Buchanan, the latter becoming managing director.

With the courage of his convictions, Francis Ley now embarked on a decisive course of action that was to see the vindication of his engineering and commercial views concerning the future for malleable iron. He selected and purchased a parcel of land in what was then the still independent township of Litchurch, his selection clearly being strongly influenced by its proximity to Osmaston Road and the railway. What must also have been an important consideration was the rapid development of housing in the nearby Rose Hill, Arboretum and Normanton areas, which would provide a ready source of labour. This red-brick explosion, as it is sometimes known, was made possible initially by the break up of old estates and land-owning families whose holdings had hitherto formed a barrier to a southward extension of Derby. Alongside this release of land was the rapid increase in demand for labour, created mainly by the railway industry. Railways came to Derby in 1839, but, a few years before, an agreement had been reached between three railway companies to focus their operations and headquarters in the town. The three companies were the North Midland Railway, the Midland Counties' Railway and the Birmingham and Derby Junction Railway, and despite the fierce competitive climate of the time they surprisingly agreed to operate from a joint station after pressure was brought to bear on them by the Town Council, which wished to avoid a plethora of stations. This influx of railway engineering provided the ingredients for industrial growth. Not only did the railways create employment on a major scale, but they also established the circumstances which attracted other commercial ventures to the area by offering a convenient and rapid method of transporting supplies and finished goods. To give an indication of the scale and speed of development of the Litchurch area, it is worthwhile recording that the population of the township at the beginning of the 19th century was less than 100 but by 1866 was around 53,000. It was in this year that Litchurch was given its own local government, and it remained an independent township until incorporated into the Borough of Derby in 1877, by which time its population had grown even further to around 70,000.

On 29 July 1873 an auction was held at the Midland Hotel by Messrs Oliver and Newbold. Lots 9, 10 and 11, collectively known as Lime Pit Close, were each described as 'a piece of exceedingly valuable land suitable for the erection of business or manufacturing premises'. The three parcels of land ran from Osmaston Road in a westerly direction between the railway lines belonging to the London & North Western Railway Co. and the Midland Railway to the south, and Black Lane to the north. It is interesting to note that at this time Black Lane was very much wider than it ultimately became and, at a width of 40ft, provided excellent access from the three plots onto nearby Osmaston Road. The area of the three plots amounted to approximately four acres, and this was the land purchased by Francis Ley on that July day in 1873. The former owners of the land were Miss Augusta Caroline Leacroft and other members of the Leacroft family.

Francis Ley was clearly not a man to drag his feet, as is evident from a drawing that exists on which is shown a series of buildings sketched on the middle plot. The drawing referred to is that which illustrated the land in the auctioneers' sale catalogue, so it is fairly safe to assume that Francis Ley had prepared his ground well enough to be able to give instructions for detailed drawings to be started as soon as he had secured the purchase. Further evidence to substantiate this is provided by an illustration of the works bearing the date 1878 which, despite some artistic licence, shows a great similarity to the original sketch that appeared in the marked up auctioneers' drawing. It must be remembered that Francis Ley was a competent engineer and draughtsman, and not only did he know the number and position of buildings that he required but he also designated their function. His original sketch defines eight buildings, comprising: offices, stables, earth closets,

'View of the works 1878.'

fitting shop, annealing shop, foundries, engine house and sand sheds, all contained within the central plot of the three.

The fact that he chose to erect his buildings on the central plot poses a question. It is obvious that he wanted the westerly plot for possible future expansion, but why did he not choose to begin his building in the logical place, on the plot adjacent to Osmaston Road? In 1873 Colombo Street (formerly Percy Street) and Malcolm Street were not yet fully developed, so it was not an issue concerned with trying to align his buildings with adjoining street layouts. There was also a parcel of vacant land lying between the line of Colombo Street and the boundary of Francis Ley's newly acquired land, this vacant lot belonging to the estate of Douglas Fox of Brighton, Sussex. Therefore, the question remains to be answered, why did he not use the plot closest to Osmaston Road which at that time was the only means of access to his site via Black Lane?

The answer to the question may lie within his reasons for selling the one-acre plot next to Osmaston Road. On 28 September 1874, just over a year after purchasing the land, Francis Ley had an agreement drawn up between himself and Henry Fowkes for the sale of the plot to the latter, who is described in the agreement as a fire grate and kitchen range manufacturer. The conveyance was not carried out until 6 February 1875, the purchase price being £1,050, but the title deeds were retained by Francis Ley.

Henry Fowkes was a prominent Derby man and, in addition to being deeply involved in public affairs, was closely associated with the local iron trades. He also became a member of the Litchurch local board and eventually became its chairman, remaining a member until the board's dissolution on 31 October 1877, after which event he joined the Derby Town Council. In November 1884, by unanimous consent of the council, he became Mayor of Derby. However, he did not manage to complete his term of office, as on 19 August 1885 he died at the age of 67. In the 1860s he had established a company for the manufacture of fire grates and general ironwork, which he operated from premises in Wellington Street, off London Road.

This profile of Henry Fowkes serves to illustrate that there must have been some degree of association between him and Francis Ley, albeit maybe only one of acquaintance. There existed much common ground between the two men, despite an age difference of some 27 years. Both were experienced in the local iron-founding industry, and they were also connected by the township of Litchurch and the borough of Derby, as in 1877 Francis Ley was elected to the Derby Town Council as the councillor for the Arboretum Ward. It follows that with all this common ground they must have been well known to each other. Nevertheless, for whatever reasons lay in the background that brought about the sale of this one acre of land to Henry Fowkes, whether it was pre-arranged or an afterthought, it had no influence on the urgency with which Francis Ley applied himself to the creation of his enterprise.

The latter half of 1873 and 1874 must have been a frantic time for Francis Ley as during this period, while acting as his own clerk of works and manager, he transformed a bare field into an operational malleable iron foundry. The financing of this project was made possible by what must have been a substantial loan from his father George, who became a partner in the business. Also in these early days he was joined by Henry Millar Gray of Duffield, who was later taken into partnership as his confidential assistant and right-hand man. It is not clear to what extent George Ley and Henry Gray lent their efforts in the period during which construction of the foundry was taking place, but such evidence that does exist suggests that the entire responsibility of seeing the project through to completion of construction and commissioning was carried by Francis Ley himself.

CHAPTER 2

1874 to 1918

THE PRECISE date on which the new foundry opened for business is not clear, but it was certainly during 1874. A number of sources quote May Day of that year as being the date on which trading commenced, but the first cash entry to the credit of the Capital Account was made on 23 April 1874. As construction work could not have begun much before the autumn of 1873, it was clearly no mean feat to have got the venture up and running within the period of about nine months. It is reputed that commissioning and initial production was largely an issue of everyone joining in and getting their hands dirty, and that included Francis Ley, and is said to have been carried out by a few well known and trusted colleagues. What is sure is that it would have been necessary to employ experienced men in melting iron and mould making so maybe a number of men from Handyside's were tempted to join him, but for many of the other processes of manufacture it would have been a relatively easy task to obtain and train unexperienced local labour.

The original factory layout can be seen in the illustration entitled 'View of the Works 1878' (see page 20) and, with the help of Francis Ley's sketch made five years earlier on the auctioneers' plan, the buildings can be identified. In the foreground behind the railway wagon are the sand sheds, obviously located to accept material direct from the L&NWR line. Behind the sand sheds lies the engine house and further back are the foundries. To the left are the two bays comprising the annealing and fitting shops. In the background from left to right are the offices, stores and stables.

From the very beginning, the proximity of the L&NWR and the Midland Railway was an obvious attraction for the supply of raw materials and the despatching of finished goods and over the years Ley's invested considerable sums of money in the construction of their own private sidings and locomotives. It is worth noting that a comprehensive study of Ley's activities in this area was made by D.B. Blackall, his work being published by the Industrial Railway Society in the early 1990s.

The first few years of business for Francis Ley's new Vulcan Ironworks was on a rather modest scale as he strove to establish his products in an industrial environment that had not yet fully accepted the engineering advantages of malleable iron. It will be remembered from earlier comments that the only technology available at that time for the manufacture of malleable iron was by the so-called European method, which fell short of guaranteeing either quality or performance, thus making it difficult to convince the customer of the reliability of the product.

In 1878 there occurred an event that is best described in the words of Francis Ley himself, 'one of those golden opportunities occurred, which, if grasped, led on to fortune'. He was making reference to the Ewart's Patent Chain Driving Belts. Perhaps the most authentic account of how the Ewart name and product became synonymous with Ley's is the report of a speech made by Francis Ley at a dinner held at the Royal Hotel in Victoria Street on 1 December 1882. Earlier that day Francis Ley had invited a few friends to look over his works and see the operation of chain making from beginning to end, and, in the evening, to dine with himself and his employees at the Royal Hotel on Victoria Street, Derby. Among the visitors were the Mayor, Mr Robert Russell, the ex-Mayor Mr Abraham Woodiwiss, Mr T. Roe, Mr W. Hobson, Mr J. Smith, Mr G. Wheeldon, and Messrs F. Hoult, T.G. Clayton, R. Speight and R. Osborne, the latter gentlemen being heads of departments at the Midland Railway. They were treated to an extensive tour of the Works conducted by Francis Ley and his right-hand man Mr H.M. Gray. A very detailed and graphic report of this tour and the following dinner appeared in the *Derby Mercury* on 6 December 1882, and, although the highly-descriptive narrative of the production scene may not mean a great deal to the reader with no experience of a working foundry, it is well worth repeating here for the sake of historical accuracy and, not least of all, for the pleasure derived from the flowery Victorian prose. For those who worked at Ley's, it will provide an insight into its history and, in some instances, an amusing look back into the foundryman's working life in the late 1870s.

The visitors were first of all taken to the moulding shop, where the business of casting was about to be commenced. To the uninitiated eye the spectacle was an impressive one. It is a thing not to be easily forgotten to take a train ride from Birmingham to Wolverhampton on a dark night, and watch the clusters of black men who surround the furnace doors and poke the fire and prod and pull about the great pieces of red hot metal which lie inside. That is a serious picture; but the casting work at the Vulcan Ironworks has a humorous aspect, which reminds one of the hungry workhouse boys in Oliver Twist, *clustering with their basins in their hands round the master in anticipation of soup. When it is decided that the molten iron in the furnace is fit to be cast a bell is rung, and the moulders, who have arranged their sand moulds in rows upon the floor, proceed to the furnace to get their supply, taking with them vessels capable of holding a couple of quarts or so, and fixed, so as to be carried conveniently, at the end of broom handles. As each man gets his allowance – and a generous stream pours out of the furnace door – he runs away to his moulds, creating, if he spills a drop on the way, a shower of those handsome sparks which one admires so much in good fireworks. When all are moving about it appears to be a difficult thing, notwithstanding the many admonitory 'Look-outs' to avoid a collision, but this was achieved on Friday and without the spilling of a single pot of metal. It is difficult to remember that the contents of these pots do in a short time become hard, cold iron, and the moulders seemed to think so too, for as one had filled his sand moulds he asked his neighbour 'Will you have a sup?' or 'Can you do with a pint of liquor?'. Nevertheless it is so, and whilst we watch the vapour which soon begins to come out of the moulds, some of the castings are sufficiently cooled, and are thrown in a heap together.*

The visitors were next shown the annealing ovens – places very suggestive of one or two punishments described in Dante's Inferno – where the cast iron is put to stew, as it were, but comes out toughened and malleable instead of tender; and they were also shown the fettling and finishing shops, the weighing and pattern rooms, and the extensive warehouses containing the varied productions of the firm.

The visit was a very enjoyable one, and the visitors could not help noticing the admirable arrangements which exist from the office downwards, the great amount of breathing space there was in each shop, and the general aspect of health and comfort – to say nothing of the smartness and good looks of the females engaged upon the works.

Soon after six o'clock a dinner was provided at the Royal Hotel to which Mr Ley had invited all his employees and a number of his friends. The room had been handsomely decorated, and the whole of the arrangements were excellently carried out. There were about 250 guests, including a number of young ladies employed by Mr Ley, and the dinner was of a first class character. The host was supported on his right by the Mayor of Derby (Mr R. Russell), and on his left by the ex-Mayor (Mr A. Woodiwiss), and amongst the other gentlemen present were Alderman J. Smith JP, Alderman T. Roe JP, Alderman Hobson JP, Alderman Sowter, Mr G. Wheeldon, Councillors Newbold, A. Woodiwiss jun., Unsworth, and Marsden, Mr W. Canning (Burton Upon Trent), Mr John West (Manchester), Mr R. Speight, Mr T.G. Clayton, Mr J. Worsnop, Mr H.M. Gray, Mr W.J. Piper, Mr W. Iliffe, Mr T. Coulthurst, Mr T. Prince, and Mr Popplewell.

The loyal toast having been proposed from the chair, Alderman Sowter (in the absence of Alderman Bemrose through indisposition) proposed 'The Army, Navy, and Reserve Forces' remarking on the honour which Sir Hy. Wilmot and Sir D.C. Drury-Lowe had conferred on their native county, and on the high degree of efficiency to which the Derby Volunteers have attained. Capt. Newbold (1st DRV) acknowledged the toast and said *though the Volunteers had no glorious victories in the field to boast of they had been qualifying themselves to be good citizen soldiers in time of need. Mr Speight proposed 'The Mayor, Magistrates, and Corporation of Derby' and in the course of his remarks said he for one was not sorry that Mr Ley had recently retired from the Corporation, for he would be able to give more of his valuable time and attention to that important industry with which all those present were so closely associated, and when the time came for him to retire on his laurels, and hand the active conduct of the works over to his son, he could give the town the benefit of his experience and business capacity. (Applause). The Mayor responded and took occasion to remark on the lamentable number of cases which came before the magistrates as the consequence of the vice of drunkenness. As to the Corporation, they had during the last 15 or 16 years done as much, if not more, to advance the interests and the prosperity of their town as any Corporation in the country. (Applause). Alderman Hobson submitted 'The health, happiness and prosperity of the Chairman', which was received with rounds of applause. He said though he had not been personally acquainted with Mr Ley, he had known him ever since he had come to Derby 15 or 16 years ago as pupil, and afterwards partner, in the eminent firm of Handyside & Co., and latterly as the head of that gigantic concern which was known far and wide as the Vulcan Ironworks at Derby. (Applause). He had that day had the privilege and pleasure of looking over those works which had been reorganised, extended and completed and, he was very pleased to see on all hands evidence of the energy, the ability, and the capacity of Mr Ley in bringing those results about. Unlike Mr Speight, he regretted exceedingly the loss of Mr Ley's valuable services to the Corporation. The toast was drunk with much enthusiasm, and Mr Ley was loudly cheered on rising to respond.*

He said this was one of those occasions which do more to cement the friendship between employers and employed than any words could express. (Cheers). As many of them were aware, it had been proposed to hold this dinner last year, in celebration of the completion of the improvements, but the Yankee furnace kicked against being run by a Britisher, and it was not until he had been over to America to see where the kicks originated that they got over its obstinacy. (Laughter and applause). They had since run it successfully very many times, and those who visited the works that afternoon had seen it in operation. Proceeding to give a sketch of the rise and progress of the Vulcan Works, Mr Ley said it was due to the kind recommendation of Mr Michael Thomas Bass that he first came to Messrs. Handyside's as a pupil. After he had become a partner in that concern he persuaded his partners to let him have a department under his own control for the manufacture of malleable castings; and the result was so far satisfactory that he commenced the Vulcan Works on his own account, though it was then a very small place for such an industry.

They got on year by year, and about four years ago one of those golden opportunities occurred, which, if grasped, led to success. He received an order for a quantity of Ewart's chain links to be shipped to Australia, and he was not aware for what purpose they were required. Shortly after that he was showing some exhibits at the Royal Agricultural Show at Bristol, and upon examining some self-binding reaping machines which were at work there, he noticed upon them a considerable quantity of chain links of the very pattern he had made for the Antipodes. He gave certain instructions to Mr Gray (cheers) to show patterns to the implement makers and quote prices. A few weeks afterwards a gentleman walked into his (Mr Ley's) office, and the upshot of the conversation that ensued was that the pattern from which the chain links for Australia had been made was the patent of an American firm represented by the gentleman, who had visited England for the purpose of introducing and pushing the article. He (Mr Ley) immediately offered to make over to the firm in question the whole of the profit on the Australian goods, but the gentleman said that was not the object of his visit. He had applied to the largest manufacturers of malleable iron in this country to take up the patent, but they had declined. The result of their further conversation was that he offered to undertake the manufacture in England if the American firm would make it worth his while to do so. A reasonable royalty was agreed upon, and from that time to this the trade had gone upward. (Cheers). The American firm had since promised to give him the working of all the patents they might hereafter bring out, besides sending him fully-worked details of their large and extensive works. (Cheers).

A great deal was said against American manufacturers, but he ventured to say there were very few manufacturers in this country who would have shown an equal amount of generosity. (Cheers). When he received from the American firm their figures and costs he was amazed, and Mr Jackson, one of the managers, could not believe they were right until he had himself been over to America to see how it was done. The result of Mr Jackson's visit was that they had improved the Works very largely and now they had overcome all difficulties, and he was happy to say that they had also been able to give a wrinkle or two to the Americans. (Applause). The only drawback to his pleasure on the present occasion was that he had just received intelligence of the death of his greatest and best friend in the United States.

In conclusion he again expressed his thanks to the company for their cordial reception of the toast. (Applause).

The Chairman then proposed 'The Visitors' and expressed his great regret that Mr Andrew Handyside was prevented by indisposition from attending. He coupled with the toast the names of Mr Canning and Mr West. Mr Canning expressed his gratification at seeing such a body of employees enjoying the company of their master and his friends, and urged the workmen to emulate the example of several gentlemen present who had risen from being working men like themselves to positions of power and influence. Mr West (who is manager of the Manchester Gasworks) urged all the employees to do that which they were directed, to do quickly and in the best possible manner, and they *would not only be helping themselves and their master, but would be assisting Derby in her competition with the world.*

Mr Clayton proposed 'Prosperity to the Town and Trade of Derby'. So long as there were such enterprising men in Derby as Mr Ley there was no fear for the progress and prosperity of the town. (Applause).

Mr Woodiwiss first responded. He urged the necessity for keeping pace with the times and said he thought this was being fairly done at the Vulcan Works at all events. He was especially pleased to notice a number of young women employed there. Derby had many important advantages and he was convinced there was a great future before the town. (Cheers).

Alderman Smith also responded, touching upon the history of the foundry industry in Derby, with which he had been acquainted for the past 50 years. He spoke of the marvellous progress which had been made at the Vulcan Works and predicted a prosperous future for them.

The Mayor in proposing 'Prosperity to the Vulcan Ironworks' spoke with admiration of the manner in which the men had faced the fiery furnace that afternoon, and said he saw displayed at the Works an amount of energy, ingenuity, and skill which was not surpassed in England. (Applause). Derby ought to be thankful to Mr Ley for introducing a new industry to the town, and he hoped that before many years had passed the Works would have doubled in extent. (Applause).

Mr Gray, in responding, said they had every reason to anticipate for the Works a brilliant and prosperous career. What would be for an ordinary man the work of a lifetime had been accomplished by Mr Ley in a very few years. He hoped the friendly and harmonious feeling shown that day might long prevail.

The evidence provided by the foregoing report of Mr Ley's speech in December 1882 leaves no doubt as to the foundation of his success in those early years. The inadvertent infringement of that American patent in 1878 went a long way to sealing the growing fortunes of Ley's up to the advent and subsequent rapid development of the automotive industry.

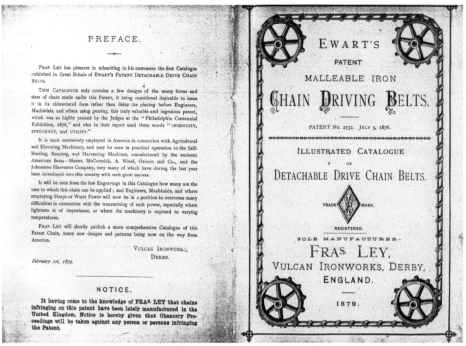

The first catalogue for Ewart's Chain Driving Belts, from 1879.

In 1879 Francis Ley produced his first catalogue containing Ewart's Patent Chain Driving Belts to coincide with the Royal Agricultural Society show at Kilburn. A preface to the catalogue brings to the reader's notice what nowadays we would call a rave review. It states: 'the ingenuity, efficiency and utility of this product as judged at the Philadelphia Centennial Exhibition of 1876.'

From a modern viewpoint it is not always easy to appreciate the significance and impact on the engineering world of the 1870s of such a development as the Ewart Chain Link. In those days it offered many advantages over the more widely used methods of transmission, such as leather or rubber belting, by providing a positive and slip-free way of getting power from the prime mover to the position where the power was required to perform a function. Although pitch chain was already in use at this time, the Ewart system also had the advantages of the ability to carry attachments, such as elevator buckets, wide range of speed, durability in conditions of dirt or elevated temperature and cheapness of manufacture. Its main area of employment at the time was in the agricultural industry, where in America it was widely used in the operation of self-binding, reaping and harvesting machines.

The mention of agricultural machines brings to light another interesting incident in the early days of Ley's. On 9 August 1881 The Royal Agricultural Society held an event at Thulston, a few miles south of Derby, but owing to very heavy rain in the afternoon the sheaf-binding trials were suspended. To pass the afternoon, the judges of implements, the stewards of the implement department and the consulting engineers to the Society decided to pay a visit of inspection to the Vulcan Ironworks owned by Mr Ley. The newspaper report in the *Derby Mercury* goes on to say:

> *This gentleman is the sole manufacturer for Great Britain, the continent of Europe, and other countries (excepting the United States of America and Canada) of Ewart's patent detachable drive chains, which form a very important constituent in the details of all the self-binding harvesters on their trial at the Thulston field.*
>
> *Although unexpected, the visitors were cordially received, and personally shown by the proprietor over these extensive works, in which the most approved Anglo-American plant is extensively adopted.*

The report goes on in fine detail to describe the self-invited visitors' tour of the works and some of the more notable remarks were:

> *'...they inspected the coremaking, which in this establishment is all done by females, a very unusual sight in a foundry'.*
>
> *'the moulding machines are a type designed and constructed by the proprietor, one, a power machine, patented by Mr Ley, turning out excellent work. It is constructed to be worked by Ewart's chain, leading from a line shafting running the whole length of the foundry. With this machine a labourer and three boys can turn out about 500 moulds in the day of 12 hours, or rather 12.5 hours, for in these works the 54 hours per week are made up in the first five days, the hands working from 6 to 6.30 on the first four days, and paying up on Friday evening at 5.30, make a holiday on Saturday.'*
>
> *'...the American system of snap flasks is adopted throughout'*
>
> *'a reverberatory furnace of five tons capacity was also inspected –*

this is the most approved type of furnace as used in the manufacture of malleable castings.'

'...the visitors spent about three hours in inspecting the works, and were much pleased with what they saw, congratulating the proprietor most heartily on his success.'

It is very clear from the 1881 and 1882 reports of visits to the Vulcan Iron-works that, from the first encounter with the man from Ewart's of America, Francis Ley had lost no time in changing his production methods in favour of those employed by the American manufacturers. It appears that the area in which the transformation had proved to be most awkward was that of melting, where it was crucial to get the metal composition correct in order to achieve all the advantages offered by the American type of malleable iron.

He always took great pains to advertise the benefits of American malleable, which does not come as any great surprise, as he had concluded at a much earlier stage in his career that a great future lay in store for malleable, but hitherto the technology surrounding the American material had not been available to him.

It would be appropriate at this stage to briefly explain the differences between European and American malleable. The malleable industry in Great Britain had generally been confined to small firms. Their attitude towards product development was, to say the least, conservative. They had neither the inclination nor the necessary scientific ability to advance the theory or the practical requirements of chemistry to lift their business out of age-old traditional methods and continued to turn out castings of indifferent quality and performance. Despite this, competition in the early British malleable industry became keen, and in attempting to keep their costs low the producers were tempted, in many instances, to purchase low grade white pig iron, the smelters of this pig iron being only too glad to off-load an inferior material for which there was little demand. It is no surprise, therefore, that the castings made under such conditions were very difficult to anneal properly and that the finished product was difficult to machine and unreliable in service. This was most damaging to the reputation of malleable and a good number of British firms failed as a result, but what was even more of a blow was the resulting erosion of confidence in the material, which effectively checked its development and growth for some considerable time.

It took many years before the prejudice was overcome and this was largely achieved through the efforts of men such as Francis Ley, who had the vision, tenacity and expertise to further the cause through the appliance of science.

In the United States of America the opposite had applied, and malleable cast iron had been the subject of a great deal of scientific study. They had started out with one significant advantage, and that was the exceptional quality and purity of their domestic iron ore, which existed in huge quantities and was ready to hand. They also had an abundance of timber for conversion to the charcoal which was used for smelting the ore. The nearest that the British industry could get to this quality of base material was to import from Sweden. With the aid of a more advanced scientific approach to the chemical control of malleable iron production, together with a total quality control concept from pattern making to finishing, the Americans were able to produce easy to machine, consistent and reliable castings.

It will be useful at this point to understand where Francis Ley stood in relation to the rest of the malleable iron industry and to spend time looking briefly at the origins of the material and how it became one of the most important engineering materials.

Malleable iron is an alloy made up principally of iron and carbon, but it is transformed from a hard, brittle, as-cast state, into a tough and ductile material by the application of heat treatment. The process of heat treating produces castings of outstanding ductility together with the valuable properties of strength, resistance to impact and corrosion and the very important feature of easy machinability. Another distinctive characteristic is that it can be cast into intricate shapes, thus giving the engineer the capacity to exercise more imagination and freedom in design work.

The French metallurgist Reaumur was the first to document the technical aspects of malleable castings in the early 1720s. He carried out a process of 'malleablisation' by packing castings in crushed iron ore and keeping them at a high temperature for a number of days. Without entering too deeply into the realms of metallurgy, suffice it to say that Reaumur's method removed the hard iron carbide from the as-cast material, producing castings that possessed qualities of ductility and toughness. When fractured under tension the surfaces of the break displayed a greyish white colour, hence the term 'whiteheart' came into being.

A century later in America, where 'whiteheart' had found only limited use, an inventor and industrialist by the name of Seth Boyden set out to popularise the material within the rapidly growing engineering industry of his home country. He was well aware of the wide use of 'whiteheart' in Britain and Europe and, with the aid of information and sample products from these sources, he set up his own foundry in Newark, New Jersey, in 1820. His primary aim was to reproduce European 'whiteheart' malleable. Between 1826 and 1832 he carried out many detailed experiments with various raw materials and heat treatments, but was never able to reproduce what he understood to be 'whiteheart' malleable. Unwittingly, Boyden had produced a cast iron that bore little relationship to the European malleable he was pursuing, but he had in fact produced an entirely new material which possessed better properties than the 'whiteheart' he had spent several years trying to emulate. Boyden, although following Reaumur's methods more or less to the letter, had ended up with a material that, when fractured, in no way resembled the characteristics of what he perceived to be European malleable. The nature of the fracture of Boyden's material displayed a dark velvety appearance and it was this feature that ultimately gave rise to the term 'blackheart'. At this stage of his work, and without attempting to experiment further with annealing procedures, the material that Boyden had produced was beginning to be taken seriously by the American engineering industry and in 1831 he was granted the first American patent for malleable iron.

Over the next 20 years, malleable iron manufacture gathered pace and, with the rapid expansion of agriculture and the railroad system across America, a firm market was established for castings in these two fields of engineering. During its infancy, some aspects of the production of malleable were, to an extent, regarded as mystical, and individual manufacturers were inclined to keep their techniques a closely guarded secret. This, for a number of years, tended to inhibit development of the material, but in the early 1880s the industry began to increase markedly in response to an unprecedented demand from railroad equipment designers in particular, and this led to the formation of many more foundries and the opening up of further development of the material.

A key element in Boyden's early work, that had apparently gone without proper consideration, was the difference in composition between American and European pig iron. It has already been noted that American iron ore was of better quality than its European counterpart. It produced pig iron containing higher levels of silicon, which is a constituent that causes more carbon to precipitate within the iron during heat treatment, giving the 'blackheart' effect on fracture test. All this work by Boyden resulted in his cast iron being generally accepted by the American engineering industry and by the 1850s its use was widespread in his native country. Such was the importance of his work in establishing the American malleable industry, that in later years in Newark, New Jersey, a statue was erected to honour his memory and achievements.

At the time that 'blackheart' malleable was taking a firm hold in America, Francis Ley was beginning his career at Handysides, but with the independent nature of the foundry industry that prevailed on both sides of the Atlantic, together with the entrenched attitudes of British foundries, it is no small wonder that it took another 15 years for 'blackheart' to gain a foothold in British engineering. It is probable that Francis Ley's first positive contact with the American malleable industry was in 1878 when he entered into the deal to produce Ewart chain belt under licence. Although it is very likely that he was well aware of the general progress being made in America, it was at a time when members of the industry were in the habit of keeping their cards close to their chests. On establishing the Ewart deal, it would not have been in the interests of the American company to withhold its metallurgical technology, and it is reasonable to assume that from that time onwards Francis Ley was set on a course that eventually led him to be able to produce the superior quality American malleable.

This short foray into the early technology of malleable iron production gives an indication of the enormous challenge that faced Francis Ley in the 1870s. Not only was he battling against a prejudice that had built up against malleable iron, but there also appeared to be a distinct lack of desire to invest in the development of the material. It is, therefore, not too surprising that the Vulcan Ironworks only progressed on a modest scale during the first four years of operation. When, in 1878, he first became involved with Ewart's of America, Ley must have been well aware of the advantages of American malleable and the difficulties of attempting to emulate their practices given

Some of the earliest engravings, made within the first five years, dated 1879.

Ewart's patent detachable drive chain foundry.

Shop for dressing castings.

the lack of resources available to him. His resolve to succeed and ability to know a good thing when he saw it drove him to grasp this opportunity to tap into the American malleable scene.

Following his fortuitous meeting with the representative of Ewart of America and the subsequent agreement for Ley's to manufacture under

View of the annealing house.

licence, it was clear that the quality, performance and reliability of the American iron would not be able to be reproduced in Britain unless the technology surrounding the American practice was made available to Ley's. This was readily forthcoming with the Americans allowing Francis Ley access to everything from information concerning chemical compositions to working practices, technical drawings and manufacturing costs. This was accompanied by an invitation to visit some of their manufacturing plants – an invitation he personally did not take up until the autumn of 1880. It will be remembered from Francis Ley's speech at the Royal Hotel in 1882 that as soon as he had received the information from America he had despatched one of his trusted colleagues, a Mr Jackson, to America in order to confirm some of the claims the Americans were making. It is clear that Mr Ley treated the affair with the utmost urgency, and such was his confidence in American malleable and the marketing opportunities that lay ahead for this material, as well as the more immediate benefits to the manufacture of Ewart chain links, that he straightaway began to modify his manufacturing methods.

The early visits to the US were made by leading foremen, but it soon became clear that the changes required to accommodate the American ways were going to be extensive. They would have, by nature, some far-reaching effects in the overcoming of resistance to change usually demonstrated by a workforce of that time. New methods demanded new training, and it was anticipated that some members of the workforce would not be suitably qualified to cope with them and that it would be necessary to bring in new blood.

Subsequent visits to the US were made by Mr Ley and Mr Gray, but on his return from the 1880 visit Francis Ley realised there was no place for half measures and immediately began to modify many of the buildings erected only seven years before. At the same time, he initiated the installation of the American methods and American-style plant and equipment. The information he brought back from his tour was in great detail, to the extent that many items and engineering devices could be constructed directly from his notebook sketches. Everything that he observed, which he thought would be of use, he measured, sketched and made calculations, employing the skills he had acquired as an engineer during earlier years. He and his more senior colleagues then set about the task of implementing the new ways, much of which was carried out by themselves on the shop floor.

As pointed out before, one of the key ingredients of American malleable was pig iron of a high level of purity, and while the European market was being searched for suitable material the ground-breaking decision was made to import American pig iron. This could only be done at certain times of the year owing to the size of vessels trading on the Great Lakes of America and weather conditions prevailing. When the first consignment of pig iron was imported in 1881 it caused quite a stir within the iron industry, which, by and large, could see neither the demand for, nor the cost effectiveness of such material.

1881 was the year when, for the first time, 'blackheart' malleable was produced at the Vulcan Ironworks. This was made possible only by employing imported American pig iron and by the adoption of closely controlled annealing methods. As referred to before, the name 'blackheart' derives from the appearance of the fracture which, due to the nature of the carbon within the material, displays a dark velvety texture. Castings made in this type of malleable are strong, tough and readily machineable, also having an ability to dampen mechanical vibration. In time, 'blackheart' was to prove an ideal replacement for many traditional forgings and was ideally positioned to take full advantage of the forthcoming development of the automotive industry.

Once embarked upon the major reorganisation of his works, Mr Ley then had the task of selling his American malleable castings and Ewart chain to a sceptical market. Catalogues were produced, mainly put together by Mr Ley, extolling the virtues of 'blackheart' malleable. In the catalogue for 1883, for instance, there appears an open letter bearing his name in which he lays down the merits of his products. Also contained within this catalogue is a picture of the Vulcan Ironworks, clearly showing a significant increase in the number of buildings.

The level of input into establishing the business, carrying out a major reconstruction and convincing a doubting industry to accept his products, all in the space of 10 years, must have demanded an enormous effort from Francis Ley. He had laboured so strenuously over this period that his health broke down. He had, however, by this time, established a company which was firmly set on the road to continued success, as trade grew steadily as the customer base widened to embrace the new malleable and Ewart chain.

The year 1883 could not have been a good one for Francis Ley. His health became seriously impaired, mainly through overwork and, whereas up to this time he had participated in practically every aspect of his business, he had to relinquish much of the day to day running to his closest colleagues. A direct result of this was to convert the business into a Limited Company, the shareholders being Mr Ley as Governing Director, Mr Gray as Works Director and some heads of departments. Strangely, Mr Ley's father George is not listed among the shareholders, but in 1883 he still appears on the letter headings alongside Francis and H.M. Gray. The depth of friendship that had grown up between Ley's and the proprietors of the American foundries was further cemented in 1886 by the Americans also taking up a shareholding in the company which, by then, was known as Ley's Malleable Castings Company Limited.

Taking up further the question of Mr Ley's state of health, it was not only the burden imposed by the commercial workload that took its toll, but also the amount of involvement he had with local affairs. Living not far from his works, first at 41 Trinity Terrace, London Road, and later at 2 Hartington

Street, he doubtless felt a sense of duty towards the community in which he lived and worked and soon became associated with local government. In 1877 he was elected on to the Derby Borough Council as councillor for the Arboretum Ward. He served on numerous committees including Baths and Washhouses, Bass' Recreation Ground, Cabs and Fire Brigade, Standing Orders and Stipendiary. He also published a pamphlet in 1877 entitled '*The Question of a Stipendiary Magistrate – A Few Facts not Generally Known*'. In this he sets down a considerable number of facts and figures surrounding the possible appointment of a Stipendiary Magistrate for Derby. Also during 1883, he received a personal set-back which to his questionable state of health would no doubt have had a considerable impact. On 7 June his mother, Sarah, died at the age of 63.

Another feature of 1883 was the purchase of a parcel of land to the north-east of Colombo Street, bounded to the south by Black Lane. Triangular in shape and measuring 1,471sq yds, this land was bought from the estate of Douglas Fox for the sum of £220 13s and was to become, some good few years into the future, the final site for Ley's and Ewart's Institute. In later years, part of this land was used for the construction of offices for the Ewart Chainbelt Company, the access to which was from Black Lane or by means of a footbridge from the Ewart's Works passing over Black Lane to enter the offices at first-floor level. These offices have now been amalgamated with the old Institute building to form the present-day headquarters for the Ewart Chainbelt Company.

As the business grew, it soon began to put pressure on the size of the original three-acre Ley's site, so between 1887 and 1889 further plots of land were purchased. These included an area lying alongside the southern edge of Colombo Street, previously owned by the estate of the late Douglas Fox, a four-acre plot known as Reeves Meadow, and a number of building plots around the junction of Vulcan Street and Harrington Street. The Colombo Street plot was later used to erect a new main entrance, an office for the Ewart Chainbelt Company and a Messroom. The plot referred to as Reeves Meadow was the original Ley's recreational ground, later to become part of the area on which the game of baseball was played and ultimately the home of Derby County Football Club – but more about that subject later. The area purchased around the junction of Vulcan and Harrington Streets, which was

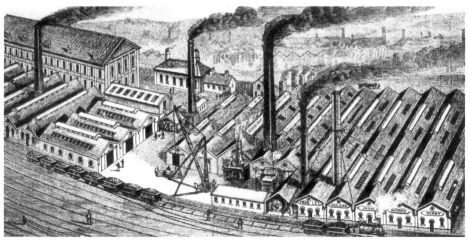

An illustration of the works from 1888.

included in an auction at The Mart in Albert Street on 15 April 1887, was used to create the Vulcan Street entrance to the works. It is likely that at the same auction a plot of land on Shaftesbury Crescent was purchased, which was later used by Mr Ley to build St Christopher's chapel.

By 1885 Francis Ley was in good enough health to undertake another visit to the US. This he used to bring himself up to date with the latest developments in the American malleable world. He also took the opportunity to gather much information on working practices and, in particular, the many small and often overlooked items that contributed towards making tasks more bearable to his foundry operatives. His interest in what might be regarded as trivial engineering devices may have been influenced by his employment of a high proportion of young people. The physical abilities of these employees would have been somewhat limited within a heavy engineering environment and any contrivance that would reduce operative effort not only benefited the user but also enabled the employer to engage juveniles, so contributing towards lower wage bills.

No sooner had Francis Ley regained his health than, in 1886, he suffered two further personal losses. On 28 January of that year his father George died at the age of 65 and 11 months later, on 23 December, his wife Georgina passed away at the early age of 40. In the space of just over three years he suffered three bereavements: his mother, father and wife, all of whom are buried in the churchyard at Barrow-on-Trent.

Within two years he remarried. During June of 1888 he was married to Alison Catherine Jobson, daughter of John Jobson of Spondon, a man also engaged in the iron business and who founded a company which later became known as Qualcast. Francis Ley took into this marriage the three children from his marriage to Georgina, Agnes aged 16, Ethel aged 15 and Henry Gordon aged 14. At the time of his marriage to Alison, Francis Ley was residing at Barrow-on-Trent Manor House, a house described as a gentleman's residence commanding an open view of the River Trent and the countryside towards Stanton-by-Bridge and Ingleby. This house, built *c.*1775, still exists but only in a truncated form as, due to an unsound roof, the top storey was removed in 1954, leaving a rather odd looking single-storey building.

Back at the Vulcan Ironworks, the business continued to grow steadily and in the late 1880s and early 1890s the output had risen to about 1,250 tons per year. Castings were being produced for the railway, agricultural and electrical industries with the Ewart chain driving belts continuing to make a major contribution to the business. The number of employees had also risen steadily from 140 at the start of the 1880s to around 200 by the end of that decade.

It was during this decade that a very interesting application of the Ewart chain belt is recorded. Since 1880, trials had been taking place in the Dover area to assess the feasibility of a Channel Tunnel. These trials had been conducted by Col. Thomas English of the Royal Engineers using a boring machine based on Beaumont's patent of 1875. This machine carried rubble from the boring head to tram wagons, by which means the rubble was removed from the workings. The rubble was transferred by a form of bucket conveyor driven by a Ewart chain belt. The same method was also used for the boring of the Mersey Tunnel. The Channel Tunnel project proved to be exceedingly slow and only achieved a distance of almost 1,500ft over a period of 14 weeks. Problems were experienced with the reliability of the boring equipment, the propping methods and, strange to relate, the number of visitors to the workings, who no doubt hindered the progress.

Throughout the 1890s and past the turn of the century, Francis Ley and his senior colleagues were still having to promote the virtues of 'blackheart' malleable iron, as is evidenced by the nature and composition of contemporary catalogues. Even in 1901 the company still felt it necessary to explain to the British engineering industry the reasons behind the enormous development and use of malleable castings in the US and the causes behind its slow take-up in this country. Ley's went to great lengths in their attempts to convince a very conservative engineering fraternity of the numerous advantages of employing 'blackheart' malleable castings in place of traditional English or European malleable or forgings. In 1901 Ley's published a catalogue entitled '*Malleable Castings – American and English Practice*' which dealt, in very precise terms, with the engineering advantages of embracing the American practices. However, just over the horizon was the engineering revolution that was to change the philosophy and fortunes of many engineering firms worldwide – the automobile was on its way.

Since Karl Benz had begun to sell his cars in 1887, followed by Gottlieb Daimler two years later, the development of the motor car had progressed at a lively pace, particularly in mainland Europe and the US, but in the UK its progress was stifled by regulation and restrictive laws. Until 1896 no vehicle was allowed to travel on a UK highway unless it was in the charge of at least three people, one of whom had to precede the vehicle, on foot, while carrying a red flag.

The first mass production techniques were pioneered in 1901 in the US by the Oldsmobile Company, followed by Henry Ford who developed these methods still further when launching his Model T in 1908. At the same time in the UK, motor manufacturing was, by comparison, on a much smaller scale and spread across many small companies, some of which initially treated the assembly of motor vehicles as more of a sideline than a core product. It was not until after World War One that mass production of all types of motor vehicles really got into its stride in the UK, and very rapidly the acquisition of a motor car became within the reach of the general public.

Ley's, with its 'blackheart' malleable cast iron, was ideally placed to take full advantage of the arrival of the motor vehicle, as this material was in many respects perfectly suited to be employed as component parts. Motor design engineers have always regarded the minimising of weight as a very important feature of a vehicle's design and performance. Among the materials available, 'blackheart' malleable, in a great many applications, offered the best option from the early days of automotive manufacturing through to the 1970s. Much of this was in the future for Ley's so to return to the closing years of the 19th century, the company was progressing steadily forward as suppliers to the general engineering industry while still enjoying the success of Ewart drive chains as one of its mainstays of production.

From the start of the company in 1874, Francis Ley had taken care to foster a culture of co-operation and harmony in his relationship with the workforce. He had achieved this through his close involvement with all matters concerning production and commerce and had always placed himself at the forefront of every aspect of his business. In 1893 his workpeople decided to recognise this by presenting him with an Illuminated Address, of which, in order to demonstrate the depth of feeling that prevailed, the words are reproduced here:

We, the undersigned, representing the employees of Ley's Malleable Castings Co. Ltd., Chain Belt Engineering Company, and Ewart's Chain Manufacturing Company, being desirous of recognising in some small way the good feeling which has so long existed between yourself and those employed by you, ask your acceptance of this Illuminated Address.

We cannot help recognising the fact that the large business in which we are engaged is the outcome of your energy and foresight, and you have spared no pains to develop and extend the Works which give so many regular and remunerative employment.

We are pleased to put on record that as an employer you have ever desired to promote our welfare in many ways which tend to our comfort and advantage. Our families also have been considered and the kindly interest taken in them, both by Mrs Ley and yourself, merits our gratitude.

During the development of your great business, our relations have been singularly free from disputes, and the good feeling and justice which has characterised your treatment of us has been the medium of promoting the harmony that exists.

We sincerely trust that our present relations will long continue; and that you may long be spared to see the further development and progress of the Works of which you may be justly proud; and

Epperstone Manor in Nottinghamshire, the home of Sir Francis Ley from 1894 until he died there in 1916.

that the unanimity and good feeling which has prevailed hitherto may long remain undisturbed and may still more be increased and strengthened.

This Address was signed by a number of senior managers and workmen and dated 26 August 1893.

The following year, Francis Ley moved house yet again. He purchased a property in the village of Epperstone in Nottinghamshire. Epperstone lies about eight miles to the north-east of Nottingham and remains today a quiet backwater of about 500 inhabitants. Francis Ley's newly-acquired residence, Epperstone Manor, commanded a frontal aspect looking south over some 70 acres of parkland while its rear elevation ran alongside the village main street opposite to the parish church of the Holy Cross. The house is of a handsome, three-gabled construction dating back to the 17th century, but the manor itself goes back to Norman times. The estate was purchased from Thomas Huskinson, a member of a prominent local family, and Francis Ley lived there until his death in 1916, after which it was sold in the following year to Stanley Bourne. Since 1954, the house and its grounds have been home to the

The works in 1895.

Nottinghamshire Police Authority, being used for offices and latterly as a training establishment.

As the output from the foundry steadily grew, together with the constant reviewing and subsequent introduction of American production methods, the requirement for more space became a priority. Further land was purchased to enable the foundries to be extended in a westerly direction and in 1889 another parcel of land was bought from the estate of Douglas Fox. This land, to the south of Colombo Street, was separated from Ley's land by Black Lane, the latter forming the northern boundary of Ley's original property.

Black Lane at this time was still some 40ft wide and created a major barrier to an extension of Ley's in a northerly direction towards Colombo Street. Up until 1899, Black Lane maintained its original width, taking a course behind the fireman's cottages in Colombo Street up to a point behind where the messroom was ultimately to be built. It then reduced in width to become a footpath running between Ley's foundries and the football/baseball ground until it joined up with Vulcan Street. The location of this plot of land fronting Colombo Street was clearly not strategic to production flow on the Ley's site but, once the restrictions imposed by Black Lane had been overcome, it allowed Ley's to extend up to Colombo Street. Some form of agreement with the local planning authority must have been arranged to allow Ley's to develop the site across Black Lane, but it is interesting to note that a wide roadway was maintained through Ley's along the course of Black Lane and between the buildings that were subsequently erected a few years after acquisition of the land. It was not until 1917 that Black Lane was officially stopped off and redirected to link only from the end of Colombo Street to Osmaston Road and was later reduced in width to its final size.

In business terms 1897 was a significant year. It was decided to reconstruct the business on a broader financial basis, and the Ley's Malleable Castings Company Ltd came into existence with a share capital of £200,000. The shares were held in their entirety by the Ley family and those who were shareholders in the previous company, so none were made available to the general public. A year earlier, Francis Ley's eldest son, Henry Gordon, always referred to as Mr H. Gordon Ley, was appointed to the position of

A portrait of Sir Francis Ley, signed and dated 1897, showing him at the age of 51.

Sir Henry Gordon Ley
(1874–1944)

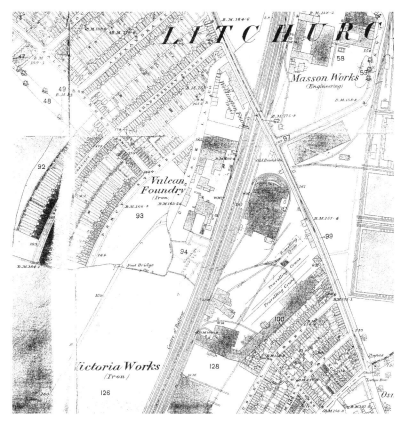

A map from 1899, 25 years after the establishment of Francis Ley's Vulcan Foundry. Note the Wellington Foundry of Henry Fowkes and Percy Street, later to be re-named Colombo Street.

assistant works manager. Born in 1874 at Aislaby near Whitby, the year in which his father had established the business, he had received his education at Repton and subsequently in Germany, where he made a particular study of analytical chemistry. He also spent some time in America studying foundry production methods, so when the time came for him to join Ley's in a practical capacity he was able to bring with him a background of knowledge which would prove to be of great value in maintaining Ley's eminent position in the malleable industry. He was largely responsible for building up a metallurgical control system and promoted the further development of the Works Chemical Laboratory which, in 1899, was considered to be innovative within the iron industry.

H. Gordon Ley must have been a well-known figure about the works even before 1896 as, a year earlier, when he attained his majority, he was presented with what is described as a handsome gift from Ley's employees at a celebratory gathering held on the Baseball Ground. 1899 brought another cause for celebration when H. Gordon Ley was married to Rhoda, the daughter of Herbert Prodgers JP, of Kington St Michael near Chippenham in Wiltshire. A point of local interest is that Rhoda was the sister of the vicar of St Bartholomew's at Elvaston at that time. The newlyweds took up residence at Willington House, Willington, which had been occupied by a preparatory school from 1875 until its closure in 1899. They remained at Willington until the early 1920s after which they are recorded as being domiciled at Lazonby Hall near Carlisle.

Two sons resulted from Ley's marriage to Rhoda; the first being Gerald Gordon born in 1902, and the second being Francis Douglas born in 1907.

H. Gordon Ley gave some of his time to military matters and in January 1900 was gazetted to the South Notts Imperial Yeomanry Cavalry. He rose to the rank of major until he was recalled from service abroad in 1916, upon the death of his father.

By 1903 the factory site had grown to about 15 acres and the firm was employing approximately 830 people. Year by year, existing buildings were extended and new buildings erected on land that had been purchased several years before in anticipation of business growth. It is interesting to note that, during the first decade of the new century, increase in production was to some degree limited by the lack of availability of skilled labour. In contemporary catalogues there appears something of a veiled apology that '*this difficulty has rendered it impossible for us to book each year more than a limited number of new customers*'. This problem seems, yet again, to reinforce the case that Francis Ley had maintained, from the very beginning, a policy of protecting his reputation for quality products by employing a selective approach to the engagement of labour. It is well known that he involved himself very closely with all aspects of production and commerce in the early years, but as his health deteriorated in the 1880s he confined himself more to the administrative side of the business. Such was the case concerning the image of Ley's projected by brochures of the time, as ample evidence exists of his personal involvement with the preparation of material for publication.

He was always very keen to illustrate the history and development of the business of which he was so justly proud and to project a message that Ley's could be relied upon to produce material of unquestionable quality by virtue of attention to detail and the application of the most up to date methods and equipment.

An illustration of his attention to detail and the culture he generated, fostered and proudly protected, is given by a letter he sent to a senior member of his staff, a copy of which appeared in a commemorative booklet in 1949:

The letter is dated 4 November 1908 and goes on to say:

> *Referring to the letter sent to the Works today, it gives me an opportunity of calling to your attention to what is a blot on your excellent business capacity. Brevity is an excellent thing but you must not go to extremes in this and curtness is as bad a fault as too much the other way, and is apt to lead customers to think you are too independent, and in these days of competition it will not do.*
>
> *Your curtness takes that indefinable shape to which a man cannot directly complain about and yet puts a man's back up. There is a sort of air 'Come to us if you like or leave us if you please'.*
>
> *When you get another ten years over your head you will more fully grasp my meaning. Take my advice and try to avoid this failing and be as diplomatic as you can. Extreme courtesy pays. Curtness never does.*
>
> *Believe me,*
> *Your old sincere friend,*
> *Francis Ley.*

The first few years of the new century saw Ley's carry out a considerable amount of building development. The site had grown to an area of about 15 acres and up to this time practically all expansion had been for production purposes. With the acquisition, some years earlier, of the parcel of land on the south side of Colombo Street, the opportunity was presented to improve and increase accommodation for the administrative staff and to provide more up-to-date employee welfare facilities.

The year 1904 saw the completion of a new messroom, an imposing building, 160ft long by 50ft wide, fitted with a fully equipped kitchen and with a capacity for 850 workpeople. By the standards of the day this must

Ley's messroom pictured in 2004, 100 years after it was built.

have been at the forefront of on-site employee welfare, and, costing about £5,000 to complete, it had clearly been designed to accommodate a variety of functions. At one end of the main hall was a roomy stage containing a grand piano, and, shortly after opening, the stage was fitted with a magnificent organ upon which daily lunchtime recitals were given. When set out for dining, the hall could hold 500 men with separate accommodation for female employees and a further separate area for office staff. Sometime during the 1920s the organ was removed and the full stage given over to presentation ceremonies and performances by Ley's Operatic and Dramatic Society.

The opening ceremony was a grand affair. Held on the evening of 5 February 1904, invitations were extended to all employees to attend a celebration banquet in the new messroom. A six-course meal was followed by toasts and speeches interspersed with entertainment ranging from organ recitals to comedy songs. The guest list included the Bishop of Ripon, father-in-law of Ethel Boyd-Carpenter who was the younger daughter of Francis Ley. The Bishop, the Rt Revd William Boyd-Carpenter, was called upon to propose a toast to the success of Ley's Works. Other local luminaries delivering speeches during that evening were Sir Clement Bowring JP, Richard Bell MP, who, incidentally, was Derby's first Labour MP, Sir Henry

Bemrose MP, Sir Thomas Roe MP and the Reverend M.H. Pitts-Tucker. An event of such splendour, attended by so many eminent Derby citizens, provides a measure of the importance of the occasion not only as an indication of Ley's standing within local industry, but of the regard in which Francis Ley was held for his concern towards the welfare of his employees.

One end of this messroom fronted on to Colombo Street and alongside this was constructed a new works entrance which, very soon afterwards, was graced by an elegantly proportioned set of wrought-iron gates announcing 'LEY'S WORKS'. On the opposite side of this new main entrance, a building was constructed that was to form the headquarters of Ley's Institute. The original institute had been built at the Osmaston end of the Baseball Ground in the area known as 'Catcher's Corner'. A crucial element of this latest building development was to align the new main entrance with the bottom of Malcolm Street. This gave anyone approaching the works an impressive long-distance view.

Having described the arrival of the new messroom in 1904, it is fitting, at this stage, to dwell for a moment on one of the best remembered and often related features of Ley's employee welfare. This concerns the coffee canteens, a description of which appeared regularly in Ley's catalogues of the time, and formed part of a description of the range of facilities provided for employees both inside and outside working hours. The section dealing with the coffee canteens reads thus:

> *Each employee entering the works at 6 a.m. during the six months ending March 31st is given a pint of hot coffee, nicely made, and a small currant or plain bun, it being felt by the firm that these, in addition to well heated workshops, enable the employees to start work on cold wintry mornings in comfort.*
>
> *The two time offices (one for the Malleable Castings, and the other for the Drive Chain Department) have each a coffee canteen attached. Trays of buns and cans of coffee are placed on a long table fixed on the side of the covered passage leading into the works, and each employee on entering takes a bun and can with him to the department in which he is working. The cans are collected at 7a.m., washed, and stored away ready for next morning's use. The coffee and bun is a great inducement to the*

employees to come at 6 o'clock in the morning. About 100 of the buns have currants in them, and the first comers can, if they desire, have these in preference to the plain buns – they appear to have an attraction for the youthful employees.'

The Ley's Institute provided a facility for the exclusive use of employees for recreational and educational pursuits. The Institute was managed entirely by an elected committee of workpeople drawn from both the offices and production departments. It contained a reading room which was provided with the daily newspapers, magazines and periodicals. Two full-size billiard tables and a miniature rifle range completed the facilities. Connected to the institute were various outdoor recreational clubs comprising football, tennis, cycling, cricket and a fishing club with its own waters. During the winter months, there existed a lively competitive atmosphere with matches in billiards, whist and rifle shooting arranged against other local Institutes. The more strenuous recreations, such as cricket and football, were played on a 12-acre field adjoining the works. During the summer months, the workpeople and their families also had access to the Derby County Football Club ground, for athletic sports and playing baseball. At this time the ground was owned by Ley's. In 1895 Francis Ley had agreed to lease the 12-acre area to Derby County. This enabled them to transfer from the Nottingham Road Racecourse where their match fixtures were being compromised by race meetings. There had been occasions when league matches had been cancelled owing to a clash of dates, and, as the Racecourse authority always held the upper hand, the football club were regularly inconvenienced. They must have been only too pleased to relocate to Ley's baseball ground where they could be assured of the support of a man of sporting inclinations. The lease granted to Derby County by Francis Ley was for a nominal amount, and together with his continued support and the flexibility he allowed in the use of the ground the football club was able to build its future on a reliable foundation. Eventually, in 1924, Ley's sold the ground to Derby County for the sum of £10,000. In the 1960s, during the Brian Clough era, Derby County once again approached Ley's for assistance with the development of a new stand. A narrow strip of land running along the rear of what was then known as the 'Pop Side' was handed over to Derby County, once more for a nominal sum of money, and as a condition of the sale the subsequent construction became known as the Ley Stand. Regrettably, over the ensuing years, this stand was re-named the Co-op Stand and finally the Toyota Stand, so severing an important historical link with Ley's who had contributed so much, in terms of generosity and encouragement, to secure the stability of the football club during its early years.

The game of baseball and its links with Ley's is a topic about which much has been written over the years, but the story of the company would not be complete without at least a brief description of how the game was established and developed in England and the part played in this by Francis Ley.

During his visits to the United States in the 1880s, Francis Ley became seriously enthusiastic about baseball and grasped every opportunity to see a game. His enthusiasm ran so deep that he was determined to see the sport firmly established in England and during the 1890s achieved a great deal towards this end by his continued support and sponsorship. In 1889 a number of exhibition games were played in England by two professional American teams, sponsored by Albert Spalding of sports goods fame. It has not been possible to establish whether or not Francis Ley had any connection with Albert Spalding while he was in the United States, before these exhibition games took place, or if the events and Francis Ley's own moves to bring the game over were merely coincidental. Whatever the background to the first games to be played over here, it is well known that in 1890 Francis

The Derby Baseball team in 1897. Back row: D. Allsop (captain), J. Evans, J. Reidenbach, J.W. Robinson, E. Booth. Seated: S. Bloomer, H. Gordon Ley, Francis Ley, H.M. Gray, Alex Langlands, T. Presbury. Seated on ground: J. Mellors, J. Saxton, W. Berresford.

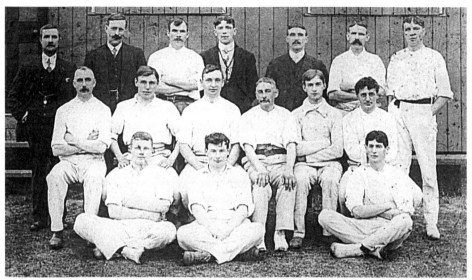

Ley's cricket team, *c*.1900. Back row: J. Moss, S. Kirkland, W. King, J. Fawcett, J. Jeffreys, J. Adams, S. Bloomer. Seated: T. Kirkham, H. Barnes, W. Matthews (captain), W.E. Dexter, J.W. Smith, H.E. Burton. Seated on ground: J. Bagshaw, F. Tapping, J. O'Donnell.

Ley prepared a section of Ley's recreation ground, complete with stands and changing rooms, and proceeded to launch the first baseball game to be played in Derby on Saturday 3 May. His team, known as the Derby Baseball Club, was fully operated and sponsored by Ley's, and at that first game the opposition was a team from Erdington in Birmingham. Francis Ley himself played a leading role by umpiring the game, which resulted in a 23–11 win for the Derby club.

As with all things he set himself to do, Francis Ley dealt with baseball in a professional manner not only by importing American kit for his team, but also by importing competent American players who also, conveniently, worked for companies in the malleable iron industry with which he had close business connections. On 1 April 1890, a legal agreement was drawn up in Cleveland, Ohio to bring over to England two experienced moulders to work in the Derby foundry and, as they were also baseball players of proven ability, to instruct the Ley's players under the direction of Francis Ley. As the following document is such an important element in the establishment of the Ley's/Derby Baseball Club it is reproduced here in full.

> *This agreement, made at Cleveland, Ohio, this first day of April*
> *1890, by and between Francis Ley of Derby, England, party of the*

first part, and John Reidenbach and Sim Bullas of Cleveland, Ohio, parties of the second part, Witnesseth:

That the said Francis Ley has engaged the said second parties to go to Derby, England, with the prospect of remaining there during the summer of 1890 for the purpose of working as moulders in the works of Ley's Malleable Castings Co., Limited, and also for the purpose of playing baseball and instructing the said Ley's baseball players under his direction, the proportionate time to be spent in either employment to be at the discretion of the said Ley and that the said Ley hereby agrees to pay the said Reidenbach monthly at the rate of sixty dollars per month and the said Bullas at the rate of fifty dollars per month in Federal currency, or its equivalent in English money, from the time said second parties leave Cleveland to the time they return, and also to pay their travelling expenses going and returning, including railway fares, ocean passages, meals while travelling by railway, and hotel bills in New York, and that the said second parties hereby agree in consideration of the above purposes of the said first party to go to Derby, England, for the purposes above stated, and to remain there during the summer of 1890, if required by the said Ley, it being mutually understood and agreed by the parties hereto that should said Ley's baseball playing venture prove unprofitable, or should the services of said second parties, either as moulders or ball players not require said Ley sufficiently to warrant him in keeping said second parties in his service through the summer of 1890, then said Ley has the option of sending said second parties back to Cleveland earlier, he to pay all their expenses and for their time as hereinbefore provided by the option as to time of service up to August 31st 1890 being with the said Ley.

Witness our hand this third day of April 1890
Signed:

- *Francis Ley,*
  John Reidenbach,
  Sim Bullas,
  Witness: O.K.Brooke.

With the inclusion of the two Americans, it was not surprising that the Ley's/Derby team became one of the most dominant members of the newly formed National Baseball League of Great Britain. Of particular concern to the other league members was the ability of Reidenbach, a pitcher of some merit, to deliver a curving ball. The effectiveness of his pitching was such that claims were made by opposing teams that his deliveries were unplayable. This ultimately led to an accusation of unfairness levelled at the Derby team for fielding a side which included the two Americans. A period of acrimony ensued, resulting in Francis Ley withdrawing the Derby side from competitive games while being in a commanding position to take the league title in its inaugural year.

Not to be outdone by the likes of Aston Villa and Preston North End who, like Derby, also fielded baseball teams partly made up of professional footballers, Francis Ley became the prime mover in the establishment of a local league comprising teams from within a 40 mile radius of Derby. Despite the unpleasantness surrounding the 1890 season, Derby continued to play against the more prominent national sides, winning the English Cup on three

Ley's Football Club, season 1909–10; semi-finalists of the Derbyshire Cup.

Ley's Football Club, season 1910–11; winners of the Derby & District League and Derbyshire Challenge Cup.

occasions, first in 1895, when the result was Derby 20–Fullers (London) 19, again in 1897, Derby 30–Middlesbrough 7, and finally in 1899 when Derby defeated Nottingham Forest 14–3.

As mentioned earlier, professional footballers played a major role during the summer baseball season and none more so than in the case of the Derby club, whose ranks included the redoubtable Steve Bloomer, of Derby County and England fame, who, at one time, was an employee at Ley's Malleable Castings.

The popularity of baseball in the UK remained high until the outbreak of World War One, after which interest in the game diminished. During the 1930s there was a resurgence of enthusiasm but this was short-lived and the game never regained the level of popularity it enjoyed during the early years of the century.

Having comprehensively catered for the recreational requirements of his employees, Francis Ley then turned his attention to providing for their spiritual needs. He purchased a 1,022sq yd vacant plot of land in Shaftes-

The Ley's Baseball Ground, leased and eventually sold to Derby County Footbal Club.

bury Crescent and proceeded to fund the construction of a church at a cost of £6,000, which, on completion, was conveyed on 30 May 1904 to the Ecclesiastical Commissioners for England and Reverend Francis Adams of St Thomas's, in whose parish it was situated. The conveyance included the unconsecrated building which, it stated, when consecrated, was to be used for ecclesiastical purposes forever.

The church was dedicated to St Christopher and the service of dedication took place in the afternoon of 13 June 1903. The preacher on this day was Bishop A. Hamilton Baynes and the subject of his sermon was, not surprisingly, St Christopher. It was recorded in the church register that the offertory at this service was £17 7s 5d, a considerable amount of money for those days – clearly the congregation must have consisted of a good number of well-to-do individuals.

The consecration of St Christopher's did not take place until 23 January 1905 and was conducted in the presence of the Bishop of Derby and the Registrar of the Diocese. The church was to be known as a chapel of ease in the new parish of St Thomas, Litchurch.

In 1908 the then Sir Francis Ley bestowed the gift of a stained-glass window, which was ultimately installed at the east end of the church after a Faculty was passed by the Episcopal and Consistorial Court in November of that year.

For many years, St Christopher's enjoyed a healthy patronage consisting mainly of Ley's employees and their families who lived in the Osmaston and Normanton areas, but in 1956 the church ceased to function as a chapel of ease to St Thomas's and

St Christopher's Church, Shaftesbury Crescent, built in 1906.

St James's Church in the village of Lealholm, North Yorkshire, built in 1902 largely with funds provided by Sir Francis Ley.

today operates as a place of worship for the Ukranian Autocephalic Orthodox Church.

In 1905, for the commitment, effort and dedication given towards creating an engineering company of national importance and for the services he unstintingly gave to his local communities and his workpeople, Francis Ley was justly rewarded by being created a Baronet. He became Sir Francis Ley, Baronet, Lord of the Manor of Epperstone, Nottinghamshire, and he adopted the motto to his armourial bearings 'Post mortem spero vitam' meaning 'After death I hope for life'. Also in this year, Sir Francis was appointed High Sheriff of Nottinghamshire.

Shortly after these honours were bestowed upon him, Sir Francis was struck down by a serious illness, the after effects of which afflicted him from time to time for the remainder of his life. His recovery time was lengthy and most of it was spent at his summer residence, Lealholm Lodge, in the village of Lealholm near Grosmont in North Yorkshire. During his enforced semi-retirement at Lealholm Lodge, as soon as he was able to move around, albeit with assistance, he supervised modifications to the house and the creation of a notable rock garden. The local church, St James's also benefited from his generosity when he sponsored internal works and improvements to the surrounding grounds. Sir Francis must have entertained special feelings for North Yorkshire, and in particular the area just inland from Whitby and along the Esk valley. It was here that he had been sent as a young man for private tutorage before entering the Royal Agricultural College, and it was here that he had returned, to the village of Aislaby, only a few miles from Whitby, to marry Georgina, his first wife.

As his health slowly improved, Sir Francis gradually eased himself back into his business life and his public duties, the latter including service as a Justice of the Peace for Derbyshire and Nottinghamshire and presidency of the Nottinghamshire Agricultural Society, but as his health remained a constant problem he spent relatively more of his time between Epperstone, his summer residence Lealholm Lodge and salmon fishing in Scotland. There is little doubt that at this period in his life, after 32 years of endeavour in industrial and public life, he must have entertained a feeling of satisfaction about the objectives and ambitions he had so manifestly achieved. It is, therefore, no surprise that having surrounded himself with a very able management team at the works, together with the up and coming presence of his eldest son Henry Gordon, he felt able and justified in spending a greater amount of his time enjoying the fruits of his labours.

It will be remembered that back in 1874 Sir Francis had sold off one acre of the original four acres of land he had purchased to Henry Fowkes. This gentleman was a prominent figure in Derby society and public affairs and at one time served as chairman of the Litchurch local board. He has the unfortunate distinction of dying while holding the office of Mayor of Derby – the only other Mayor up to that time to die during his year of office since Robert Hope in 1777. His passing occurred in August 1885 and for the 11 years up to this time he had conducted his business of ironfoundry from the one acre bounded by Osmaston Road, Black Lane, the railway and Ley's foundry. He operated under the name of Henry Fowkes & Co., Wellington Foundry, their speciality and main line in business being domestic firegrates.

Upon Henry's death, the foundry passed into the hands of his two sons Henry and Francis. In May 1890 Francis died, after which Henry junior's wife Ellen Jane helped with the running of the business. In 1908 Henry and his wife decided to wind up the business, which had been in continuous operation on its present and previous site in Wellington Street for about 57 years and at its peak was employing approximately 70 workers.

A conveyance was drawn up and signed on 24 June 1908 when Sir Francis bought back the one acre for the sum of £2,175, which was to be shared equally between Henry Fowkes and his wife Ellen.

Thirty-four years had passed since the 28-year-old Francis Ley had sold this one acre of land, and during this period he had managed to accumulate land amounting to some 17 acres of production area with options on further land for possible future expansion.

The acquisition of the Fowkes one acre in 1908 was not of immediate benefit to the Ley's operation as it was clear, even at this stage, that all future development of production would take place at the opposite end of the site. In 1912 a further parcel of land had been purchased from the London & North Western Railway Company, which gave Ley's the ability to expand the foundry buildings that ran alongside the Baseball Ground. The extension to this foundry did not materialise until 1917, and as the former railway company owned the remainder of the land up to a footpath that ran from Harrington Street across to a footbridge over the main railway line it was clear that the L&NWR held the key to any further expansion of Ley's on their existing site.

From 1905 until the foundry extensions of 1917, there appears to have been little in the way of major building projects. Some existing shops underwent minor changes and extensions but the one exception during this period was the building of a water tower. The tower was 80ft high to the base of a 25,000 gallon capacity water tank. At its highest level it bore the Ley's Works sign on all four elevations and very soon established itself as a familiar Derby landmark. The water tank was automatically kept full at all times with water pumped up from a 550ft deep artesian well situated close-by the tower. The height of the tank provided a high pressure water supply to hydrant and sprinkler systems and also acted as a back-up to the town water supply.

In a working environment such as Ley's, the likelihood of an outbreak of fire was an ever-present threat. Some of the buildings, in which the risk of fire was greatest, were constructed entirely of iron and steel. In the locality of the melting furnaces the roofs were higher and the spans greater in order

The water tower in 1906.

to confine a fire, or at least to slow down its rate of spread. Ley's, right from its earliest days, recognised the high cost of disrupted production and wherever practicable took steps to avoid such occurrences. This was seen, for example, in the duplication of essential services by the installation of stand-by boilers and engines. By the same token, fire precautions were treated with an equal level of importance resulting in the firm forming its own fire brigade. The brigade was made up of employees who lived close by the works in what were known as the 'Fireman's Cottages'. These dwellings were situated between the main entrance on Colombo Street and Black Lane, all being fitted with an alarm system to summon the men to an emergency. The fire brigade engaged in regular drilling and incident practice and were an efficient and effective body of men who, along with the company, took pride in their ability, equipment and not least of all in their appearance. Their professionalism was rewarded in 1939 when the brigade were winners of the All England Challenge Bowl under the leadership of their superintendent, Sam Beards.

One further building extension is worthy of mention. Due to the increase

Ley's Fire Brigade on parade after dealing with a fire in the pulverised coal plant. Back row: J. Gould, M. Furlonger, R. Richardson, R. Heed, G. Cory, J. Sawyer, S. Beard. Front row: A. Calville, J. Hughes, W. Wood.

Ley's Fire Brigade,1939 winners of the Championship of all England Challenge Bowl. Back row: A.E. Carvell, A.H. Green, F.S. Richardson, L.L. Beards, G.W. Ferguson, J.W. Collins, A.H. Heed. Front row: J.J. Hughes (sergeant), E.G. Dadge, S. Beards (superintendent), L. Middleton, J.W. Gould (second officer).

in business activity the already limited office accommodation was put under further pressure. At around the time of the water tower being built, the width restrictions imposed by Black Lane were lifted. This made it possible for the general office to be extended over the old boundary with Black Lane and towards the recently built messroom. An illustration of 1908 clearly shows the enlarged office, and an accompanying description, unacceptable by modern standards, states that '*the ledgers and day books are kept by female clerks, whilst the more intricate statistical and cost books are kept by male clerks*'.

The sequence of some of the building extensions that took place around this period suggest that Ley's took some time to assess their plans for the future. The original foundry lay alongside the boundary with the ex-Fowkes one acre, but there would have been little sense in extending the foundry operation towards the immovable barrier represented by Osmaston Road. It took two years, the demolition of some ex-Fowkes buildings and the erection of some new buildings before, in 1910, the old Fowkes site was given over

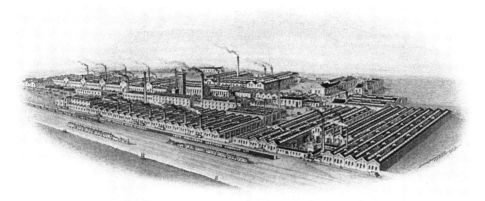

An illustration of the works in 1908.

to the centralisation of machining and assembly of Ewart products. Apart from some minor building and improvements to ancillary activities during the few years leading up to the beginning of World War One in 1914, there is little evidence of any intention of major development. However, it is reasonably safe to assume that the close commercial relationship that existed between Ley's and the L&NWR must have provided a fair degree of confidence for Ley's that future availability of land was virtually assured. As early as 1908, there must have existed a level of understanding regarding the future acquisition of land from the L&NWR as the development and capital investment made by Ley's gave every indication that the operation was on course to expand, and that a move to a larger site was never an option.

For a number of years, the southern boundary of Ley's followed the angle of the L&NWR sidings line from the main railway line to a point just north of Vulcan Street and in line with the Normanton end of the Baseball Ground. These sidings included an engine shed and a turntable and were in continual use up to 1923, at which time several railway companies amalgamated and the old L&NWR sidings became surplus to requirements.

From the earliest days of Ley's, the connection to the adjacent main railway line had played a major role in providing the company with a ready means of receiving raw materials and despatching finished goods. It is even said that most of the building materials used to construct the works in 1873–4 were delivered to site by rail. Initially, raw materials such as coal, sand, limestone and particularly pig iron were all delivered to site by rail. The latter material, as mentioned in a previous chapter, was imported from

The Ewart Chain Fitting Shop in 1910.

America, and was shipped in consignments of up to 2,000 tons at a time. Transported from Liverpool to Ley's by rail, it was then off-loaded in Ley's sidings by hand and stacked in large neat piles which covered a considerable area of the works yard. Such large stock piles were necessary to cover for the winter period when economic shipping of American pig iron was not possible owing to the St Lawrence seaway being frozen. This practice continued until 1938 when the main supply of pig iron was switched to UK sources. To accommodate the rail traffic, Ley's systematically developed its own sidings network in line with the growth of the site, employing, initially, a steam-driven cable winching system for moving wagons around the works. From 1923 onwards, locomotives were used ranging from, firstly, a home-made petrol-electric to, finally, a Bagnall diesel-electric purchased in 1963. Coal, of course, was the primary source of power for firing furnaces and raising steam. It was received by rail and man-handled in a similar manner to the pig iron. Lump coal of specified sizes was stacked in neat piles to avoid breakage and loss of burning efficiency. In 1926 Ley's built their first pulverised coal plant when coal, still delivered by rail, was then able to be loaded directly on to conveyors from drop-bottom or hopper type wagons before being elevated into large cylindrical silos.

The despatching of finished goods by rail was never a function of significant proportions and only in the case of major consignments to single customers were castings despatched by wagon directly from the works. Nevertheless, much use was made of the railway carrier road collection system until the 1920s when door to door road transport began to gain precedence. By 1940, bulk railway despatching had virtually come to an end.

At the peak of its activity in the late 1940s and early 1950s, Ley's sidings were handling up to 200 wagons per week, but this was followed by a steady decline as the economics of road transport became more favourable and on-site mechanical handling methods improved. The sidings were finally closed to traffic in 1973.

During the years spanning World War One, life at the foundry seems to have continued much as before, with little evidence of manufacturing being directed towards the war effort. It is likely, however, that in the latter part of the war, when military mechanisation began to gain momentum, Ley's would almost certainly have been involved in the manufacture of components for

The main entrance, Colombo Street, from the 1914 catalogue. On the right is the messroom and on the left is the drive chain department. At the bottom of the roadway is the Ley's general office.

military vehicles. In 1914, eight furnaces were in operation, ranging from 6 to 10 tons capacity. Each furnace was capable of delivering three or four charges of molten iron per day and, when tapped, produced a continuous stream of molten metal at which the moulders would stand in line with their hand ladles at the ready. Maintaining a continuous stream of metal was a critical affair, as once the correct temperature and chemical composition had been reached it was essential to get the iron into the moulds as quickly as possible. It was a rare occasion for a stream to be interrupted and the frantic activity on the moulding shop floor at tapping time could still be witnessed through to the 1950s.

An upturn in production demand towards the end of the war is evidenced by an extension to the foundry building. Carried out in 1917, it contained two additional melting furnaces. All the melting furnaces at Ley's were of American design and patent and were of reverberatory type, and were supplied with wind from a blowing engine situated adjacent to the main steam engine house. At this time the moulding shops covered an area of

Ian Forbes Panton.

Ian Panton at his desk in the old General Office.

about four acres and around 550 men and boys were employed in these shops alone.

By far the most significant contribution to the war effort was the number of Ley's employees who answered the call to arms and volunteered for service in the armed forces. It is sad to relate that 40 men were lost. Subsequently a memorial tablet bearing their names was erected in Ley's messroom, together with memorials to Maurice Aden Ley and Christopher Francis Aden Ley who also lost their lives. Fortunately these memorial tablets still exist and are kept in store in Derby's Industrial Museum. It is hoped that at some time in the future they will once again be on display. In the meantime, it is fitting that the names of those who gave their lives are recorded at the end of this book.

In June 1915 Ian Panton, who had been at Ley's for three years as an accountant and was ultimately to become the general manager, wrote to Sir Francis for guidance regarding the provision of equipment for the Ley's men who were willing to join the local Home Guard unit. In response, Sir Francis

Sir Gordon Ley unveiling a memorial tablet to Ian Forbes Panton. Mr Francis D. Ley is standing behind Sir Gordon.

Christopher Francis Aden Ley (1893–1918) was killed in a flying accident.

Maurice Aden Ley
(1895–1914) was
killed in action.

explains that he would be willing to provide uniforms only for Ley's men and these would comprise cap, trousers, overcoat and tunic belt, but not boots. The latter item, he felt, would inevitably be used for everyday wear. He went on to draw a comparison with a similar situation which had arisen some years earlier. He was referring to the Boer War (1899–1902), when Ley's raised a full company of 100 men. They were provided with a full kit, except for rifle and bayonet, at a cost to Sir Francis of £4 per man.

The period covering World War One was a particularly tragic time for the Ley family. Maurice Aden Ley, who was the youngest son of Sir Francis's marriage to Alison, was killed in action near Ypres in Belgium on 1 November 1914; he was only a few weeks past his 19th birthday. At the time, he was serving as a 2nd Lieutenant in the East Kent Regiment attached to the 1st Battalion Lincolnshire Regiment. The day before his death, 31 October, became known as Ypres Day, to commemorate the culmination of the first battle of Ypres, and marks the event when the German Army made a major effort to break through the British lines to the east and south of Ypres. Despite huge losses on both sides and the giving of some ground, the British managed to steady their position around Ypres. Notwithstanding this major confrontation, the exchange of artillery and small arms fire and sporadic attacks by the Germans continued unabated until the 11 November. It was during this period when Maurice Ley fell. He is buried in the White House Cemetery just a few miles to the north-east of Ypres, close by the village of St Jean.

On 17 January 1916, Sir Francis Ley, 1st Baronet of Epperstone Manor, Lord of the Manors of Epperstone, Nottinghamshire and Lazonby, Staffield, Glassonby, and Kirkoswald, Cumberland, died at the age of 70 as a result, it is said, of heart failure. The deceased Baronet was removed from his home at Epperstone and taken to Lealholm Lodge, his estate in Yorkshire. The funeral took place on Friday 21 January, after which he was interred in the churchyard of St James' in the village of Lealholm. It was manifestly appropriate that his final resting place should be in the village in which he had chosen to have his summer residence and in a part of the country that clearly meant a great deal to him. In the preceding years, he had played a leading role in the establishment of St James's chapel of ease in Lealholm. Up until 1902, the people of Lealholm were expected to worship at St Thomas's in the nearby parish of Glaisdale, but, as an alternative, services were occasionally held in Lealholm village school. Although land to build a chapel of ease was made available by Viscount Downe as early as 1881, it was not until 1901 that the foundation stone for St James's was laid. The following year, on 13 October, the new church was consecrated by the Archbishop of York. Sir Francis had been the main benefactor for the church, and from the very beginning of building work he had made funds available for such items as the bell, pews, lectern, pulpit, choir stalls, reredos and floors. On visiting the church nowadays, one will still see ample testimony to his benefaction, and, to his memory, a stained-glass window was installed in the wall above the altar. In later years a further stained-glass window was placed in the wall behind the font, and this was dedicated to the memory of his wife Alison, Lady Ley, who died in 1940. The latter window was donated by Agnes Willis Ley and Ethel Boyd-Carpenter, Sir Francis's daughters by his first marriage to Georgina Townsend Willis. Also in this church is a tablet to the memory of those who died in World War One, and inscribed upon this tablet are the names of Sir Francis's two sons, Christopher and Maurice.

Sir Francis was succeeded by his eldest son Henry Gordon who, at the time of his father's death, was serving abroad as a Major in the Territorial Forces Reserve. For many years Sir Gordon, as he had become, had been involved in military matters and had originally been gazetted to the South Notts Imperial Yeomanry Cavalry (later known as the Notts Hussars) in 1900. Educated at Repton and in Germany where he studied industrial chemistry, he had maintained his military activities along with his responsibilities within Ley's business, together with an active participation in public affairs. His involvement in the latter included serving as a JP for Derby, Derbyshire and Cumberland. He also took a special interest in the St John's Ambulance Brigade when he became Superintendent of the Derby Division at its formation in 1899 and remained in that post for a good number of years thereafter.

Before the death of his father, he held the position of vice chairman at Ley's and prior to the outbreak of war was intimately involved with the day to day running of the foundry. As Sir Francis, owing to his deteriorating health, had taken a less demanding role in the business over the few years preceding his death, the transfer of company leadership went ahead smoothly. On his return from the army, Sir Gordon, aged 42, took over as governing director and set about applying his past industrial experience in the specialisation of metallurgical control, bringing to bear a new emphasis on establishing improved quality control techniques. He was also well acquainted with American practices in the malleable industry, having studied them in detail a few years earlier. It was, therefore, something of a seamless change as far as everyday life at Ley's was concerned, with all the methods and practices established over the years of operation under the guidance of Sir Francis carrying on much as before.

But World War One had not finished with the Ley family, as on Saturday 16 March 1918 Christopher Francis Aden Ley, a Captain in the South Nottinghamshire Hussars, was killed in a flying accident while attached to the Royal Flying Corps. He was the elder brother of Maurice and was 24 years old at the time of his death. He had previously served in the Gallipoli campaign during 1915. Born at Barrow-on-Trent in 1893, he was the only other child of the late Sir Francis and Alison, Lady Ley, and is buried alongside his father in the churchyard at Lealholm, Yorkshire.

CHAPTER 3

1918 to 1938

FOLLOWING the depredations of World War One, the years between 1918 and 1925 saw little physical change to the Ley's site other than further consolidation of the Ewart's arm of the business at the Osmaston Road end of the works. The production flow at Ley's remained south to north, with bulk raw materials arriving by rail alongside the foundries and finished goods ending up in the shipping room. This department effectively formed the boundary between the Ley's and Ewart operations, and was conveniently situated close by the main Colombo Street access to the site.

The works in 1918.

The inside of the
messroom in 1920.

Although there was little change to the site, some significant administrative changes took place during 1918. The Ewart side of the business had been introduced to British industry in 1879 when Francis Ley issued his first combined catalogue covering Ley's Homogeneous Malleable Castings and Lifting Appliances together with a separate section dealing with Ewart's Patent Driving Belts. Referred to in the early days as the Chain Belt department of Ley's, it had, nevertheless, always been treated domestically as a separate concern, having its own offices and administrative staff and with machining and assembly confined to buildings which were entirely separate from the malleable castings workshops.

It was a natural course for Francis Ley to have taken to complement the manufacture of drive chain with the construction of conveyors and elevators, and in 1880 he designed, manufactured and sold his first conveyors to the Nine Elms Gas Works, London, under the banner of the Chain Belt Engineering Company. A further 39 years were to pass before, in 1918, the Ewart Chainbelt Co. Ltd was established as a private limited company through the amalgamation of Ewart's Chain Manufacturing Co. and the Chain Belt Engineering Co. Both of these companies had been owned by Sir Francis, and upon his death in 1916 they passed into the ownership of Sir Gordon. By 1919, Ewart Chainbelt were occupying offices alongside the main Colombo Street entrance in the building previously occupied by Ley's Institute, with the manufacturing shops covering approximately a further two acres in the area through to Osmaston Road.

Another administrative innovation that occurred in 1919 was the introduction, by Sir Gordon, of an employee profit-sharing scheme, thought to be the first of its kind in the industry. In his relationship with the workforce, Sir Gordon had carried on where his father had left off by continuing the policy of fostering close contact with them and maintaining a keen sense of responsibility towards their well-being. To receive a financial share in the good fortunes of the company was warmly welcomed by all employees and through the ensuing years of operation the announcement of the amount of profit to be distributed among the workforce during the run-up to the Christmas holiday was always eagerly awaited. As well as benefiting the workpeople at a time of year when, for many families, the cash was most needed, it was also aimed at creating a greater and more direct interest in the performance of the company by generating a more responsible attitude towards personal endeavours.

It was also in 1919 that some members of Ley's staff, having theatrical inclinations, formed Ley's Operatic and Dramatic Society. They did so with the full support and sponsorship of the directors of the firm, and many of the 'on-site' facilities and skills were made available to them. These included joiners to construct scenery and electricians to take care of sound and lights. At this point in time the organ, originally installed soon after the messroom was built in 1904, was removed, opening up a stage of adequate proportions for the productions envisaged. The formation of this society proved to be very popular and soon attracted members from most departments of both the offices and the works.

For the first two years of its existence, the society produced plays, starting with *Old Pals* and *Ferrills Fix* in 1919, following up with *Steeplechase*, *Waterloo* and *Tom Cobb* in 1920. In 1921 the society ventured into the world of opera with a production of *Pearl the Fishermaiden* and in 1922 *King of Sherwood*. Each year brought a fresh production of opera or drama, and in some years both, until 1928, from which date the society specialised in light opera.

Up until his death in 1944, Sir Gordon Ley remained the society's patron, supported by a full committee headed by its president, Mr Francis D. Ley. Throughout its existence the society donated its profits to local charities, the main beneficiary being the Derbyshire Royal Infirmary, and by 1938 the total amount raised had reached the sum of £590 11s 9d, a creditable amount in those days when it is considered that such an amount would have purchased a suburban semi-detached house.

The performances generally ran over five nights, and, to take an example production of *Good-Night Vienna*, performed in 1938, the cast, chorus and dancers numbered 44, with a back-stage team of seven, all supported by a London costumier and a 16-piece orchestra made up of local musicians. The profits from this particular year's production were donated to the Derbyshire Royal Infirmary Extension Fund.

Like most enterprises undertaken by Ley's and its employees, they were embarked upon with a high level of commitment and professionalism. The Operatic and Drama Society was no exception and continued its good works up until the 1950s when interest declined and it became more difficult to attract home-grown amateur talent.

From 1920 and up until 1925, it was business as usual at Ley's with little in the way of major new building. The site area, however, was now approximately 30 acres with ample space available for extension. Production of malleable iron castings had by now fallen into seven distinct customer categories. These were the general engineering trades, agricultural engineers, automobile engineers, electrical engineers, railway carriage and tramway work, shipbuilders and, of course, links for Ewart Chainbelt.

The year 1926 brought with it a major expansion programme including an entirely new foundry, a pulverised coal plant, annealing shops and pattern shops. Such was the magnitude of these additions that production was increased by 100 tons per week. Also at this time an imposing new main office was erected fronting on to Colombo Street.

The new 1926 foundry, as it became known, was a complete departure from any previous industrial construction at Ley's. The building itself was of unusual design for the period having a high castellated roof-line of seven pitches giving a high level of overhead light and ventilation. It was 360ft long and 165ft wide with perimeter walls fitted with three rows of glazing, all of which had adjustable opening gear. Not only was the building at the forefront of industrial design, but so were its contents, among which were the overhead cranes, general handling equipment and tractor type sand-slingers.

Concurrent to the building of the 1926 foundry was the installation of a pulverised coal plant. As the name implies, this plant produced coal in a very fine powdered form. This was then blown along pipes to fire the furnaces, resulting in greater melting efficiency and a more economic use of fuel. Advanced for its time, this coal pulverising plant was, in 1926, the largest of its kind in the British Isles. So successful was this new method of firing that subsequently the annealing ovens were converted to take advantage of this fuel.

The large scale expansion of Ley's in the mid-1920s appears to have followed a policy of long term planning incorporating firstly, the acquisition of land, and then when capital reserves had accumulated to the required level to release these funds to finance the expansion of production and

The old general office in 1923.

Ley's main office, Colombo Street, pictured in 2004, 79 years after it was built.

The new general office, built in 1925.

administrative facilities. Debt incurred through borrowing, it appears, was not to be contemplated.

The new Main Office, erected in 1925, was designed and fitted out to reflect the prominent position that Ley's had secured in the world of engineering. The architecture was of an imposing style and no doubt gave visitors the impression that they were about to enter an establishment of consequence and high standing. Passing through the portal, one would emerge into an oak-panelled entrance lobby to be greeted by a uniformed commissionaire and then be shown into one of a series of small but comfortable interview rooms. Beyond the entrance lobby were two large oak-panelled offices for use by Sir Gordon and his second-in-command. The offices provided for his co-directors were well appointed but not fitted out to such a high level of quality, nevertheless, they were good for their day. The ground floor general office was a revelation for the staff. They had been transferred from cramped quarters close by the workshops to an office which provided generous amounts of centrally heated space and was reminiscent of a modern dance hall, with its single span, curved and glazed ceiling. Above the offices of the senior directors was the boardroom, again oak-panelled and overseen by a portrait of the founder. This impressive room and the offices of the senior directors immediately below, overlooked a newly planted rose garden. One wonders whether this was an innovative move to promote an atmosphere conducive to constructive contemplation.

Having increased output by 100 tons per week, it followed that other sections of the works had to expand their capacity. Such was the case with the annealing shop where a further two ovens were installed. A sizeable extension was made to the pattern shop to house a new wood pattern department at first floor level, while the ground floor was occupied by new sand preparation equipment and an extension to the electrical department. The remaining processing shops were able to increase their capacity either by additional small items of plant or by increasing man hours worked. By this time Ley's was occupying a site of 30 acres in area and employing in the region of 1,500 workpeople.

Another interesting and notable engineering feature was the installation of Stirling boilers. These were attached to the new 1926 foundry furnaces and utilised the waste heat from them, converting it into steam. The steam was then used to drive generators in a nearby powerhouse. Eventually, when this generating system was extended in later years, any power generated that was surplus to Ley's requirements was sold off to the Derby Generating Company for use in the national grid.

In the closing years of the 1920s, business at the foundry was going from strength to strength, the new extensions were coming on line and there was every indication that a bright commercial future lay ahead. For Sir Gordon, however, domestic affairs were not running quite so smoothly. In 1927 he was divorced from Rhoda after 28 years of marriage. This marriage had produced two sons and a daughter; Gerald Gordon, born at Willington on 5 November 1902, Mary Rhoda, born on the 8 April 1906 and Francis Douglas, born on 5 April 1907.

Gerald, educated at Eton and New College Oxford, where he gained a BA in agriculture, did not take up a prominent role in the affairs of the business but served as a non-executive director for 33 years until his retirement in 1978. He also pursued a military career, serving in the Duke of Lancaster's Own Yeomanry from 1927 to 1939 and then with the Derbyshire Yeomanry, Royal Armoured Corps (TA) for the duration of World War Two. He was

Baseball Ground

1912

1917

1926

LEYS

Osmaston
Road

Institute

Firemen's
Cottages

Ewart
Chain Belt

Main
Entrance

Messroom
1904

Main
Office 1925

1885

1890

1926

The works in 1927.

Gerald Ley, the eldest son of Sir Gordon Ley, photographed in 1936 at age 34, eight years before he succeeded to the baronetcy.

awarded the Territorial Decoration. He married, on 19 February 1936, Rosemary Catherine, formerly the wife of Harwood Cotter and younger daughter of Captain Duncan Macpherson RN, of Somerset. From this marriage to Rosemary he had three daughters, the first being Elizabeth Bridget Rhoda, born in 1937, who at the age of 28 married Roger Humphrey Boissier, CBE, the younger son of Ernest Gabriel Boissier, DSC, of Derby. The second daughter, Annabel Alison, was born in 1939 and in 1960 married David Eric Cramer Stapleton, the elder son of Edward Eric Stapleton of Knockrobin, Co. Wicklow. The third daughter, Caroline Sheila, was born in 1943 and in December 1975 became the Countess of Lonsdale when she married the seventh Earl of Lonsdale.

Sir Gerald, as he became in 1944, had taken up residence at the family estate in Cumberland and, on becoming the third Baronet, took on the title of Lord of the Manors of Lazonby, Staffield, Glassonby and Kirkoswald. He served as High Sheriff of Cumberland in 1937. In 1956 his marriage to Rosemary ended in divorce. In 1958 he married Grace, daughter of Harold Foster of Pershore, Worcestershire, but this second marriage also ended in divorce in 1968. Sir Gerald was the archetypal country gentleman, managing his estates in Cumberland and combining a keen interest in fishing and shooting together with a great enthusiasm for railways. This zeal for railway

Lazonby Hall in Cumbria, the home of Sir Gerald Ley.

matters led him, in 1966, together with a small group of like-minded enthusiasts, to purchase from British Rail, for the sum of £4,500, the famous A4 Pacific locomotive *Sir Nigel Gresley*. This eminent locomotive, which had been destined for the scrapyard, was subsequently returned to its former glory and is now based at the North Yorkshire Moors Railway. Sir Gerald lived until 1980 when on the 24 March at the age of 77 he died at his home,

Shirley House, near Brailsford, built in 1939 by Sir Francis Ley.

Lazonby Hall in Cumbria. Some time after his death the house was sold but the estate remains, to this day, within his family.

It was in 1928 that Sir Gordon's second son, Francis Douglas, at the age of 23, joined the family firm. He had received his education at Eton and Magdalene College, Cambridge, where he gained an MA. One of his first assignments for the company, and for the benefit of his industrial education, was to spend six months in the United States studying the latest production techniques being employed in the major malleable iron plants. On his return to the Derby foundry, he familiarised himself with the day-to-day operation of all the departments, applying, where appropriate, the knowledge he had gained in the United States, while all the time building up and honing his managerial experience. Throughout his time learning the business, Francis Ley, as was the case with his father Sir Gordon, was surrounded by a board of directors comprised of men of undoubted capability and loyalty who had dedicated themselves to the furtherance of the company culture. The workforce in general reflected this attitude of goodwill between men and management which, together with the expertise and disposition of the senior personnel, ensured that succeeding generations of the Ley family were fully exposed to the doctrine so successfully established and fostered by Sir Francis and Sir Gordon.

In 1931, on 25 June, Francis Ley was married to Violet Geraldine, the eldest daughter of Major James G.T. Johnson DSO of Foston, Derbyshire. Three years later, on 12 June 1934, Ian Francis was born, followed in 1937 by the birth of a daughter, Susan Alison.

After living for some time at The Close, Ednaston, in 1939 Francis Ley purchased two fields from the Walker-Okeover estate at Osmaston on which to build a new home, the site for his proposed house being situated on the edge of the village of Shirley. The house, aptly named Shirley House, was designed by George Eaton, a prominent local architect, who did some notable works in and around Derby including offices for Rolls-Royce and the fondly remembered arcade for the Midland Drapery in East Street.

Ley's now entered the 1930s with the family succession assured and the demand for their products rising annually. The return on the capital investments made on new plant and equipment in the second half of the 1920s was materialising and capital reserves were steadily mounting until, at the very beginning of 1934, Ley's were ready to embark on another major expansion programme. As mentioned earlier, the amalgamation of the railway companies in 1923 had rendered the old L&NWR locomotive shed and sidings redundant, thus assuring Ley's of an adequate supply of land for the foreseeable future. It was on this parcel of land that work began, at the end of 1933, on the construction of a foundry of similar size and capacity to the 1926 foundry. In addition to this development, Ley's built an adjoining process shop comprising trimming, cleaning, annealing, grinding, straightening and shipping departments. This was the first departure from the traditional work flow pattern that had existed since the company was established and was the precursor for all future work flow development of the site. Alongside this new foundry a pulverised coal plant was built to serve two new melting furnaces and the new annealing ovens, and, to accommodate the increase in throughput, a new core shop and adjoining sand plant were also constructed.

During the first week in January 1934, a sod-cutting ceremony took place

A sod-cutting ceremony, with George Ford, the oldest employee, Francis D. Ley and Sydney Banks, the youngest employee, in January 1934.

presided over by Francis Ley, who by then was a director of the company. The honour of cutting the first sod fell to George Ford, the employee with the longest service, and Sydney Frederic Banks, one of the firm's youngest employees. Also in attendance at this informal ceremony was the works manager Mr W.T. Evans, metallurgist Mr A.E. Peace, the architect Mr Richardson and Mr G. Gee the builder. After completion of the ceremony, Mr Ley presented George Ford with a gold sovereign and young Sydney Banks with a half sovereign.

This new production unit was originally named the 1934 foundry, but soon became known as 'Z' foundry, as ultimately all shops at this end of the site came to be designated. Building work covered approximately three acres of ground, was completed in just over six months and provided work for approximately an extra 500 men.

In the previous year on 3 May 1933, Ley's was honoured by a visit to the works from the Duke of York, later to become King George VI on the abdication of his brother King Edward VIII in December 1936. At the time of his visit the Duke was President of the Industrial Welfare Society. In this

The visit of the Duke of York in 1933.

Thomas Jerram in conversation with the Duke.

THIS PLATE
WAS CAST BY
HRH
THE DUKE OF YORK
WHEN HE VISITED
LEYS WORKS
MAY 3 1933

The plaque cast by the Duke of York while on his visit to the works in 1933.

capacity he was to show a great deal of interest in Ley's Institute and the other facilities provided by the company for the benefit of its employees.

On his arrival at the works he was greeted by Sir Gordon, Mr Francis Ley, Mr Ian Panton, Mr E.N. Wood, and Mr W.H. Atherton. During the course of his tour of the works other employees presented to the Duke included Mr W.T. Evans, the works manager, and Miss Jessie Joyce, supervisor of the core-making girls. Miss Joyce, who had been with Ley's for 36 years, had recently been invited to unveil a tablet at the Derbyshire Royal Infirmary to mark a donation of £1,000 made by the workers at Ley's from their profit-sharing fund. This donation complemented the sum of £400 contributed annually to hospital funds by the company.

The secretary of Ley's Institute, Mr J. Evans, was also presented to the Duke, along with the boys Thomas Hayes and George Harris, both of whom had previously attended the Duke of York's holiday camp.

An interesting discussion took place in the wood pattern shop when the Duke recalled that the son of Mr Thomas Jerram, an employee in that department, had a son who at the time was engaged as second butler in His Royal Highness' household. The Duke remarked that he was pleased to report that Mr Jerram's son was giving every satisfaction in his duties.

The works tour schedule had been arranged to coincide with the tapping of a furnace in the Old Foundry, and it was here that the Duke participated in the casting of an iron plate to commemorate his visit. Happily that plate has survived the years and remains in the possession of the Ley family.

At the conclusion of his tour the Duke was entertained to tea by Sir Gordon, after which he was given a rousing send-off by Ley's employees assembled in the works yard and by local residents who lined the streets nearby.

Ley's site now extended southward as far as a footpath that linked Coronation Street with a foot-bridge that crossed the railway and joined up with Cotton Lane. In later years this footpath was eliminated and access to the footbridge was via a new footpath from the end of Princes Street. This came about when Ley's acquired a further parcel of land, triangular in shape, which took the southern boundary of the site to its final position, running on a line from the end of Princes Street to the railway lines. It will be of interest to readers who still remember Ley's site to note that the roadway into the

A consignment of castings leaving Ley's sidings in 1933.

works from 'Z' end entrance gates ran along the same line previously occupied by the original footpath from Coronation Street to Cotton Lane.

The successful development of the business throughout the 1920s and 1930s was in no small part due to the strength and dedication of the senior management of that period. In fostering the business ethics established by Sir Francis and ably continued and reinforced by Sir Gordon, this team of senior managers was responsible for the significant expansion of output in the decade between 1925 and 1935. Under their custodianship, Ley's moved to the forefront of their industry, eventually becoming the largest malleable iron producers in Europe. However, in 1935, the company unexpectedly lost a most outstandingly successful member of its senior team. Ian Forbes Panton, the general manager and director, died suddenly of heart failure at the age of 46. On Wednesday 8 May he had spent a normal day at work but during the evening while taking a stroll alone in the garden of his home, Willington House, he collapsed and died. The following day the *Derby Evening*

Telegraph described his death as 'Derby's severe loss', which gave an indication of the esteem in which he was held, not only by his colleagues and workpeople at Ley's, but by the many organisations he supported and was actively involved in within the community of Derby.

At the time of his death he was just one week away from being elected president of the Royal Institution for the Deaf and Dumb (as it was then known), and had, only the day before, toured the institution with his wife. He was also a member of the board of management and chairman of the house committee for the Derbyshire Royal Infirmary. He held the presidency of the Derbyshire League of Industry and was an ex-president of the Derby Rotary Club. The village of Willington also gained from his beneficence towards a number of activities within that community.

Ian Panton had joined Ley's in 1912 as a chartered accountant from Edgbaston and after only five years rose to the position of director and general manager. In time, he was also made a director of the Ewart Chainbelt Company. In his 23 years at Ley's he had clearly made a major contribution towards the advancement of the company and his untimely death doubtlessly left a deep sense of loss at the company as, by all accounts, he was universally loved and respected by all. Such was the level of respect accorded to Ian Panton, that a memorial service was held at St Christopher's Church on the Saturday following his death. The church was full to overflowing and the eulogy was given by the Archdeacon of Derby. Also on this day, a further service was held in the messroom at Ley's, attended by 700 members of the staff and workpeople. A further 1,200 workpeople were assembled in the yard outside and listened to the service through the aid of loudspeakers.

Three months later, a bronze memorial tablet was unveiled at a ceremony led by Sir Gordon Ley. Many ex-employees will remember this tablet as being situated on the outside of the messroom perimeter wall. This tablet is now in the safekeeping of the Derby Industrial Museum. Fourteen years later, in the 1949 brochure celebrating 75 years of business, he was still lauded as a major contributor to the success of the company and was remembered by the following words: *'a man who was always ready to lend a hand in times of need, a loyal friend, a wise counsellor, generous to a degree, slow to find fault, ever ready to impute the best motives in the action of others'*. He was clearly a man who possessed many fine qualities.

The development of Ley's during the 1930s was driven mainly by an increase in demand from the rapidly growing automotive industry. Motor vehicle design and development was also demanding increased performance from components and malleable iron castings were not excluded from this requirement. Ley's response to this was to develop a modified 'blackheart' malleable iron which became known as 'pearlitic' malleable iron. This material had been under development by Ley's laboratory staff for some time and its specification, which included a modified annealing cycle, was finally granted a patent in October 1935. It gained its name 'pearlitic' from the nature of a specimen fracture which, when polished, gave an appearance reminiscent of mother-of-pearl. In later years, further development of heat treatment techniques gave rise to 'pearlitic' materials of enhanced properties and performance and these were known by their registered trade marks of 'Lepaz' and 'Lemax'. Ley's were now able to market a comprehensive range of ferritic and pearlitic malleable irons and by doing so could satisfy the performance requirements demanded by most engineering industries. In particular, it gave the automotive engineer the ability to choose a grade of malleable iron to suit specific applications. In addition to the increased focus on producing alternative grades of malleable iron for the burgeoning automotive industry, Ley's technical staff had also developed improved materials for Ewart links during the mid-1930s, as well as exercising an on-going responsibility for continued improvements in chemical composition and quality control methods for melting and annealing.

The building programme carried out in the mid-1930s, together with the introduction of the new material grades just described, effectively set the seal on all future site development at Derby.

It was recognised that as product demand would inevitably rise and the availability of land for expansion was running out, it would soon become essential to look for alternative means of taking the business forward. The commitment made, in terms of capital resources, to provide additional manufacturing capacity was clearly not of a short term nature, and mechanisation in the iron casting industry was still very much in its infancy. Therefore, the utilisation of the remaining land by further expansion of foundries and process shops was along traditional lines, giving the business an opportunity to obtain a reasonable return on its capital investment while

The works in 1935.

North Hykeham. Nellie Tucker on her first day at work, age 14, with Jack Bainbridge.

The North Hykeham works in the 1960s.

gaining time for planning a move towards mechanisation and the necessary reorganisation this would cause.

1937 and 1938 brought about the final foundry extensions comprising four additional furnaces of similar design and output to those previously installed in the 1934 'Z' foundry. The last piece of land of effective area had now been consumed, but it was during the construction of this latest foundry, named 'Z8' foundry, that Ley's gained valuable additional capacity by the purchase, during 1937, of Harrison & Company, a malleable iron foundry located at North Hykeham, a few miles west of Lincoln.

Harrison & Co. was established in 1874 to make engineering castings. They began their business on a site in the city of Lincoln and eventually, in order to expand their capacity, they opened a branch works in Station Road, North Hykeham, in 1910. In 1922 they closed down their city site and moved their headquarters to North Hykeham.

Another milestone in the history of Ley's had occurred in January 1937 when, with the agreement of all the shareholders of Ley's Malleable Castings Co. Ltd and Ewart Chainbelt Co. Ltd, all the issued shares of these two companies were acquired by a newly registered public company going under the name of Ley's Foundries & Engineering Ltd. The nominal capital of this newly formed company was £1 million, comprising 450,000 preference shares of £1 and 2.2 million ordinary shares of 5 shillings. The directors of

Ley's Foundries & Engineering Ltd were Sir Gordon Ley, who at the time was living at Kings Sombourne in Hampshire, Francis Ley of Ednaston, Ernest Wood of Derby and William Atherton of Derby. Maurice Stevens of Derby was appointed secretary.

The Massey Ferguson tractor. The rear axle cases were made at North Hykeham.

CHAPTER 4

1939 to 1950

B Y THE outbreak of World War Two in 1939, Ley's output had risen to 350 tons per week and, as with all Britain's industry, it was then essential to begin making preparations to safeguard that output, and the people who were employed in achieving it, against possible enemy action. All the usual black-out measures were adopted and many air-raid shelters were built for shop floor workers and staff. These shelters were well scattered about the site and of limited capacity in order to minimise casualties in the event of an attack against the works. Apart from an air-raid shelter built under the main office rose garden, the remainder of the shelters were at ground level and constructed in such a way that, in the event of receiving blast from a nearby explosion, the entire structure would move en-bloc rather than disintegrate. At any rate, this was the theory. Fortunately the theory was never put to the test, although it came very close to being tested on 21 August 1940 when bombs fell around the Shaftesbury Crescent area, badly damaging a number of houses and the Osmaston Stand at the Baseball Ground. Only one bomb fell on Ley's and, from the photographic evidence available, it appears that it fell on the very end of the 1926 foundry, taking off part of the steel and concrete roof and blowing out most of the glazing from the south end of that building. Relatively little disruption to production was suffered and no casualties were reported. Had the bomb fallen a few feet further south it could have caused considerable damage to an electrical generating house which would have had serious consequences. Considering that the Luftwaffe had good aerial photographic intelligence, with accompanying text to assist them in locating Ley's Works, it is remarkable that such a well-documented and prominent target did not attract more attention from enemy aircraft than it in fact did. It is interesting that the aerial photograph used by the Luftwaffe was identical to a photograph that appeared on postcards sent through the post by Ley's as acknowledgements to enquiries during the late 1920s and early 1930s.

GB **6**, BB 17, Nr. 14: Groß-Tempergießerei Ley's Mallable Castings Co. Ltd. in Derby.
Großes Schmiedeeisenwerk im Südosten der Stadt.

A picture of Ley's used by the Luftwaffe during World War Two. (*Derby Evening Telegraph*)

A good number of employees became members of the Home Guard, and a contingent from the company distinguished themselves by carrying off a rifle shooting trophy in 1943. This achievement is not too surprising as, for many years, Ley's Institute had run a rifle shooting club which had proved to be a popular pastime for many employees. Its range was latterly located on the top floor of the stores 'A' building. Alongside stores 'A' stood the water tower which, with its 80ft high all-round external platform, provided an excellent position for observation and fire watching.

By way of further contribution to the war effort, Ley's manufactured numerous castings for military hardware applications. Prominent among these were castings for tracked vehicles such as tanks and Bren-carriers. High

A Mulberry Harbour. Ley's manufactured parts for the two artficial harbours used at Omaha and Gold beaches during the Normandy Landings in June 1944. Mulberry 'A' at Omaha was destroyed during a severe storm which lasted for four days, 19 to 23 June 1944, and was used for only 10 days. Mulberry 'B', at Gold beach, was in constant use up until the capture of the major ports of Antwerp and Cherbourg in August 1944.

The Bren gun carrier. Ley's was a manufacturer of tracks for this military vehicle.

volumes of track tread plates and sprockets were manufactured and assembled, and special production facilities were set up at both the Derby and North Hykeham Works to accommodate this and other war department requirements.

Ley's, along with neighbouring foundry Qualcast, were involved in one of the most outstanding engineering projects of World War Two. In 1944 the

Ley's Home Guard unit with their rifle shooting trophy.

two companies were engaged in the manufacture of linking and fastening equipment used to connect steel and concrete pontoon or caisson units. Each of these units could weigh up to 7,000 tons and when assembled formed the artificial harbour known as Mulberry. The Mulberry harbour played a crucial role in the support of allied forces after the 'D' Day landings in Normandy in June 1944 and was described by General Dwight D. Eisenhower as 'a real contribution to history'. Mulberry was an outstanding achievement of engineering ingenuity and organisation and, as one of the great stories of World War Two, is excellently portrayed in all its detail in a book called *Mulberry – The Return in Triumph* by Michael Harrison. This book was published in 1965 and contains a dedication to Colonel V.C. Steer-Webster OBE who was one of the main contributors to its design and ultimately to its successful application. Colonel Steer-Webster lived at Blagreaves Hall in Littleover and up to the outbreak of war had developed his engineering career with the Royal Aeronautical Establishment and the Experimental Engineering Department of the war office. He was, therefore, well qualified to take charge of the planning of Mulberry from its concept, through its technical design and development stages and on to its deployment off the Normandy coast where it kept open, in all weathers, the essential supply line to more than a million personnel of the allied forces. The Mulberry harbour project would obviously have been heavily shrouded in secrecy during its planning and construction, which may account for the difficulty in securing hard evidence linking Ley's and Qualcast to the project, but given the long association that Colonel Steer-Webster had with Derby, together with his engineering background, he must have been well aware of the capabilities of the two companies to fulfil the requirements demanded by the Mulberry project. Colonel Steer-Webster was awarded an OBE in 1944 and made a Freeman of the City of London in 1951. He continued to live at Littleover until his death in February 1970 at the age of 72.

During the war years, the government, having learnt from the experiences of World War One, took control of many aspects of British industry. In order to satisfy the demands for personnel and equipment to conduct the war, industry was controlled by the separate ministries of supply, labour and production. This provided the government with the power to direct and co-ordinate the national manufacturing resource towards the varying needs and circumstances of domestic and military requirements.

Most of the skills that existed in the engineering industry were retained to ensure continuity in the progress of technology which through the demands of war tends to accelerate at a more rapid pace than during peacetime. On the other hand, there was also a demand for engineering skills within the armed forces and to satisfy this the government allowed the trade unions an active role in the process of 'labour dilution'. This was a method by which the resource of skilled labour could be apportioned to satisfy the demands of both industry and the armed forces.

In many areas of government and industrial management, unions were still regarded as somewhat problematical, but the overiding aim of having them had to be the avoidance of industrial disruption which could result in damage to the war effort. To ameliorate the attitude of suspicion which, in those days, generally surrounded the relationship between government, industry and unions, Winston Churchill brought into government Ernest Bevin in the post of Minister of Labour. As a committed trade unionist and leader of the Transport and General Workers Union, Ernest Bevin proved to be the right man for the job. His loyalty to Churchill and the pursuance of the war was total, but he also used the opportunity to bring about a number of reforms in factory life concerning, for instance, the conditions of work, the rates of pay for women and the setting up of welfare schemes. He also promoted the use of joint production committees as a forum for management and unions to discuss the many aspects of a company's performance.

A product of the wartime policies emanating from the Ministry of Labour was to give the trade unions a much greater profile within the industrial landscape and, as a result, union membership and influence increased significantly. It was not unheard of for strike action to be taken during the war years, despite this being illegal, but thankfully these incidents never took on major proportions.

Ley's, being among the more enlightened employers when it came to employee welfare, was not unduly put out by this upward shift in union activity and influence. The company had always enjoyed good relationships with its employees and had, from the very beginning, encouraged a policy of allowing workers direct access to management. In addition to this important communication link, the company had, over the years, installed a number of facilities designed to enhance the welfare of its workers. As far back as 1899 a benevolent fund was set up to provide succour for cases of prolonged sickness and hardship, and as part of this scheme three fulltime nurses were employed to tend to the needs of employees and their families. Soon after the death of the Founder in 1916, his widow Alison established the Francis Ley Memorial Fund by means of a gift of money, the income from which was used to send convalescent workers and their families to seaside resorts to aid their recovery. Messrooms had long been in existence where workers could obtain cheap subsidised meals. The institute was another valuable contribution to worker welfare and provided a full range of indoor sports and social activities. In 1919 a profit-sharing scheme was introduced with payments originally being paid to employees each August to help with their holiday expenses, the balance being paid at Christmas time. Participation in profit sharing was open to all employees over the age of 18 who had completed a full year of service with the company. These were some of the significant ways by which Ley's attended to the welfare of their workers, but there were many other instances of unrecorded acts of benevolence that came about as a result of the policy of direct access between men and management, and of the goodwill that existed between them. Therefore, during the war years there were no pressures or demands from the Ministry of Labour or the unions that Ley's had not already made provision for, or, alternatively, if changes were deemed necessary these could be easily absorbed into their long established welfare facilities.

As was to be expected, workers in non-reserved occupations were either conscripted or they volunteered for service in the armed forces, and this dilution of the workforce was compensated for by the employment of women, where appropriate, and by the introduction of extended working hours. As the demand for war materials gained momentum, Ley's met the challenge by making efficiency improvements and the working of longer hours at the Derby Works, but over at North Hykeham, where land was available, considerable building extensions were undertaken. Much of the war time production consisted of a range of castings for military vehicles, some of these varying little from those supplied to the peace time automotive industry, to components for tracked machines such as bren-carriers and tanks. The output from the North Hykeham works, always known locally as 'The Malleable', more than doubled during the war years, but one of the main problems of that period, and for some years after the war, was the recruitment of labour. Owing to its rural location, North Hykeham experienced great difficulty in recruiting labour, but eventually this was resolved by the building of two hostels to accommodate about 160 migrant workers, this number amounting to approximately a quarter of the total workforce at that time.

During the war, Francis Douglas Ley, the younger son of Sir Gordon, played a leading role in ensuring that the company met its commitments, but he also, like his predecessors, made his contribution to the military scene through his service with the Derbyshire Yeomanry, reaching the rank of major and ultimately being awarded the Territorial Decoration. By the outbreak of war in 1939, he was occupying the position of joint managing director and his father, Sir Gordon, was taking more of a distant overseeing role, much as his father had done before him. Sir Gordon no doubt kept a steely eye on business proceedings firstly from his home at Kings Sombourne in Hampshire and then from his Scottish residence at Strathtay in Perthshire.

The manufacture of tank and Bren carrier track wheels and sprockets during World War Two. (*Derby Evening Telegraph*)

Sir Francis D. Ley
(1907–1995)

It was here at Strathtay in the spring of 1944 that Sir Gordon became ill and subsequently moved to a nursing home in Inverness where, on the 27 April, he died at the age of 70.

Coincidentally, this was the age at which his father, Sir Francis, had died, and likewise Sir Gordon had, throughout his working life, applied an equal level of endeavour and dedication to both the business and his public duties. As far back as 1899, he had been appointed a Derby Borough Magistrate and had then gone on to become a Justice of the Peace, a position he retained until the late 1930s. For many years he was the Superintendent of the St John's Ambulance Association, but his interests also extended to sport, and at various times he held the posts of treasurer of the National Baseball Association and director of Derby County Football Club. Through his connections with Cumberland as Lord of the Manors of Lazonby, Staffield, Glassonby and Kirkoswald, he was also a Justice of the Peace for that county. During the time that he resided at Furze Down, Kings Sombourne in Hampshire, he was, for a period, Master of the Tedworth Hunt.

His first marriage to Rhoda lasted for 28 years and was ended by divorce in 1927. He was remarried within the same year to Mabel Annie, daughter of Sir Philip Brockelhurst, but this marriage also ended in divorce 11 years later. In 1939 he entered into his third marriage, on this occasion to Dorothea Gertrude who was a daughter of Charles Gray of Anerley and formerly the wife of the second Baron Borwick.

A memorial service for Sir Gordon was held at St Christopher's church in Shaftesbury Crescent on Saturday 30 September 1944, and some time later a tablet to his memory was raised by the workpeople of Ley's and Ewart's bearing the apt inscription, '*In remembrance of his constant interest in their welfare*'. This tablet is also in the safekeeping of the Derby Industrial Museum.

Less than a year after the death of Sir Gordon, the war in Europe came to an end and Britain entered, what is generally referred to as, a period of austerity. Six years of war had been a huge drain on Britain's resources. With the ending of hostilities, the government introduced a number of measures to ensure that the main industrial thrust was towards the exporting of its products in order to bring in much needed overseas currency. These measures, however, did not have a major impact on the post-war production levels at Ley's, as by this time the bulk of the company's output was directed into the automotive industry which at the time was one of the largest exporting sectors of Britain's manufacturing base.

Thoughts now turned to the reorganisation of the Derby works. This was in anticipation of an increase in demand which was expected to materialise once the government decided to lift restrictions on industry and allow the domestic market to be satisfied. After six years of war and a similar period of austerity, the home market was more than ready for its many demands to be met. As Ley's was becoming increasingly involved with the automotive industry it was clear that many changes would have to be effected to enable the company to meet the demands of its customers as they themselves were preparing to move up a gear by increasing mechanisation and productivity.

When it came to plant development, Ley's followed their tried and trusted method of closely examining the advances made in the American malleable industry. Teams of senior personnel paid a number of visits to the US and, with the added impetus of a newly created development department at the Derby works, began to put together a plan for the future reorganisation and updating of the Derby site. One of the major challenges of this exercise was the avoidance of any form of disruption to the existing production capability. As there was no substantial area of land available, the development plan had clearly to be conducted in a very carefully controlled and systematic manner.

It was perhaps appropriate that with the onset of mechanisation, which by its very nature heralded a watershed in the history of the company, that 1949 should mark its 75th anniversary. The occasion was celebrated in a number of ways, among these being a dinner held in the messroom on the evening of

The works in 1948.

5 February 1949. All employees with over 21 years service attended this 'Jubilee Dinner', which occupied four hours and included long service awards of clocks and watches followed by entertainment. Commemorative brochures were made available in which historical milestones were described and illustrated. A conspicuous feature of the brochure was a demonstration of the excellent relationship that prevailed between the employees and the directors by the publication of a letter dated 1 April 1946, addressed to the board and signed by the works convenor. It is reproduced here in the form in which it appeared in the jubilee brochure of 1949.

Dear Sir

At the Shop Steward's Meeting, held on April 1st 1946, the following resolution was passed unanimously:-

We would wish to place on record our deep appreciation of the generous spirit which has actuated the Directors of Ley's Malleable Castings Co. Ltd., particularly in regard to several matters appertaining to the welfare of the employees. In the first place and quite spontaneously the Directors have increased the weekly pensions paid (as a gift, not by contributory scheme) to those employees who have retired due to old age, and we all realise what a blessing this will be to them.

Second, the Directors have evinced a great interest in the success attained by Derby County F.C. and have made it possible by mutual agreement and without detriment to production, for those employees who wished to attend important League Matches and Cup Ties to do so.

Since Derby County F.C. have qualified for the Cup Final the Directors have further displayed their generosity by offering to reimburse 300 of the employees whose names have been drawn for Cup Final Tickets, and also by meeting the expenses of the travelling involved.

Other examples will be cited, such as the fact that for the annual week's holidays the Company pay to the workpeople their average week's earnings over the year, which is much in excess of the timeworker's rates.

In addition to this a Profit-sharing Scheme operates for all employees and each Xmastime the Directors arrange a party for all employees children and distribute gifts to them. There are several Memorial and Benevolent Schemes which enable employees who temporarily break down in health to be sent to the seaside. It is only to be expected that the workpeople fully appreciate such gestures, and through the medium of the Work's Convenor and Shop Stewards wish to take the opportunity of thanking the Directors, not only for their generosity, but also for the interest they are taking in the welfare of the workpeople.

Such goodwill as is being fostered can only react to the benefit of employer and employee alike and we respectfully suggest that the spirit displayed at Ley's Malleable Castings Co. Ltd. should serve as an example to be followed by other companies throughout the country.

Signed: C.H. Hudson Works Convenor.

When it is considered how, in later years, this relationship in many sectors of British industry declined to one of a confrontational nature, it serves well to remember that, in the case of Ley's, the legacy of co-operation and consideration must have been at least partly responsible for avoiding the more hostile relationships experienced in these other areas of industry.

CHAPTER 5

1950 to 1981

THE FIRST significant step taken in the modernisation of foundry practices came in the form of the 1950 Mechanised Foundry. Built on a site previously occupied by a link foundry and No.6 furnace, this venture into mechanisation was modelled essentially on current American practice. Consisting of a continuous conveyor carrying moulds from moulding machines through the casting and cooling processes to knock-out, it represented a principle of design that was to be followed, developed and refined over the next two decades. Another first for Ley's in the construction of this new foundry was the adoption of Duplex melting, whereby primary melting was carried out in a cupola before transferring the molten metal into an electric arc furnace for chemical analysis and temperature correction prior to casting. As the forerunner of future mechanisation schemes at Ley's, the 1950 foundry not only established a principle of design, but it also produced on-going benefits in other directions. In the British foundry industry of 1950, it is probably true to say that the majority of moulds, although machine rammed, were still being put on to the foundry floor to await casting with metal supplied from a single batch melting system. Such methods were obviously labour intensive, high in manual effort and vulnerable to quality fluctuations. With the introduction of mechanisation and the continuous and conjoined processes of moulding and melting, less manual effort was involved, quality control was more easily exercised and the general management of labour was more effective. One other point deserves a mention, that being the social image of foundry work. After the war, as the British economy began to grow so did the demand for labour, which naturally gave the job seeker the luxury of choice. Foundry work was not among the most attractive means of earning a living having earned for itself a reputation for arduous and dirty working conditions. Therefore, any improvement in this image was clearly welcome. This was one of the more intangible features of mechanisation in the foundry but there is no doubt that with its introduction, and the accompanying improvement in the working environment, the difficulty with recruitment of labour was largely averted.

1954 saw the introduction of another benefit for the workforce. This time it was timed to coincide with the firm's 80th anniversary. It was a scheme designed to enable employees under the age of 55, and with at least 21 years service, to purchase a car of their own choice with an interest-free loan provided by the company. Certain conditions applied, these being that the loan must not exceed £700, the car to be purchased had to be manufactured by a customer of Ley's and the loan had to be repaid over a period of four years, out of the employee's wage packet. If the employee died during the period of the loan then the surviving spouse would only have to repay half of the remaining loan. With such generous terms the scheme proved to be very popular and ran for a good number of years. Many employees took advantage of the offer and in later years the qualifying conditions were relaxed somewhat to allow even more employees to take advantage of the scheme.

Despite the fragility of global politics during the 1950s, the future for Britain and its industries held a healthy growth potential in the satisfying of both export and home market demand. Early in the decade the post-war period of austerity came to an end and Britain still had at that time a Commonwealth of Nations as eager as its domestic market for consumer goods. With such a huge potential market, the automotive industry was forecasting a bright and prosperous future. These forecasts were obviously transmitted to the suppliers to the auto manufacturers, and Ley's, like most others, began to build up their production capacities to meet the estimates for future demand. There followed a period when there was an almost continuous need to be planning for greater output and improvements in manufacturing efficiency. Ley's problem was lack of space in which to build new production units. This problem was resolved by the systematic replacement of the old manual processes, which formerly occupied excessive amounts of space, with the installation of modern methods and equipment. Annealing was one such example, whereby the old pulverised coal fired furnaces would take over a week to anneal a batch of 'blackheart' castings, but this could now be achieved in 48 hours with electrically heated furnaces.

Working to a pre-determined plan of the final layout of the next phase of mechanisation, the old processes and service departments at the Osmaston end of the works were replaced or relocated to create the space required for what became known as the 1958 Foundry. As with all Ley's engineering projects, the concept, planning, installation and commissioning was carried out by their own technical and engineering staff.

This new production unit was a complete foundry in its own right, taking in raw materials for melting at one end and despatching finished castings at the other. It had a capability to turn out 500 to 550 tons of castings per week on a two shift system, the type of casting ranging from small engine components to rear axle housings. Complete with its own sand preparation plant, core shop, 'blackheart' and 'pearlitic' annealing ovens, this foundry was virtually self-contained and proved to be highly successful over its operational life of almost 30 years. Casting first commenced in January 1959 and a year later this foundry was described in a trade journal as *'providing a lasting tribute and monument to the many whose efforts have been directed towards producing what surely ranks among the world's best foundries.'*

The undisputed success of the 1958 Foundry laid the foundation for the future reorganisation of the remainder of the site. The engineering principles established by this project proved to be sound in practice and provided a design concept that was to be followed in a number of forthcoming projects both at Derby and North Hykeham.

Another design concept was secured at this stage when it was decided that any future melting plants would be situated centrally on the Derby site. Although amounting to some 40 acres in area, the site was elongated, its length being about seven times its width, which precluded a uni-directional work flow. It was, therefore, always accepted that, with a large range of castings spread over several different grades of material, a proportion of the output would always have to be transferred from one end of the works to the other for heat treatment and processing. The most economical way in which this was achieved was by a series of trailers hauled by Massey Ferguson tractor, known to all at Ley's as the 'wagon train'.

Having established the principles that would surround any future development, Ley's continued into the 1960s with confidence in the apparent unassailability of the domestic automotive industry on which they had now become so dependant. A demonstration of this confidence was the building of a new office block and laboratory to accommodate the works staff. A part of Ley's history had to be demolished to make way for the new building, this being the original 1874 general office which, at various times, had been occupied by Sir Francis Ley, Sir Gordon Ley and many other senior executives. Built to the best standards of the time, the new building provided accommodation for approximately 100 works administration and technical staff and was completed in 1961. A few years later, in September 1968, the top floor was severely damaged in a fire that was described in the local press as Derby's worst fire of that year. The blaze originated in the air conditioning system on the top floor which gave it the means to spread quickly along the ductings and ceiling void. The fire was spotted in the early hours of the morning by a member of the night shift and was immediately recognised as being beyond the ability of the works fire brigade, who called in the Derby Borough Brigade. Fire damage was confined mainly to the corridors, but most of the offices suffered smoke and water damage. Fortunately, the laboratory spectrographic equipment, which was located on the ground floor and provided analytical information for the furnaces, escaped damage, and the only loss to production was for a short period while the electrical supply was re-established.

Ley's had always been active in the field of research and development of the mechanical properties of malleable iron. Over the years they had progressively improved heat treatment techniques to advance and extend the range of these properties to produce materials that gave the customer the ability match a material more closely to the purpose for which it was intended. Such materials, for example, were known as 'Lemax' and 'Lepaz', but in the early 1960s a new material appeared in the market to present a challenge to some of the traditional grades of malleable iron. This newcomer was known by various names; Spheroidal Graphite (SG), Nodular, or Ductile

The works
in 1962.

Iron. It derived its name from the nodular form of graphite that formed in the metal while solidification was taking place in the mould. This metallurgical process was brought about by the addition of magnesium to the molten iron before casting, resulting in a material whose properties closely resembled those of certain grades of ferritic and pearlitic malleable. However, unlike malleable, where all grades require a form of heat treatment to achieve ductility, certain grades of SG iron could be used in the as-cast form. This feature, of course, was of great commercial significance for not only was it to have a marked impact in the malleable market but it also provided the auto designer with an alternative to steel forgings, this latter point also opening up a new market for the foundry industry. A considerable proportion of the cost of producing malleable iron castings was in the energy requirement for heat treatment, and this cost was on-going regardless of volume, therefore, the appearance of SG iron, the production of which was within the scope of many smaller foundries, created something of a threat to Ley's market. In the past, the very high capital cost of plants to produce malleable castings in volume had been an effective deterrent against the smaller players in the industry, but SG had now opened up a new area of competition for the high volume producers. It was clearly essential that Ley's would have to respond to this threat, and they immediately started experimental work to produce the new material.

In terms of foundry practices, there were some fundamental differences between malleable and SG which gave rise to some early difficulties, but, despite these and the control systems required to keep the distinction between the two materials during their progress through the factory, SG eventually became a significant contributor to Ley's overall output of castings for the automotive trade.

It must have been recognised during the early 1960s that, together with the continuing need to modernise to increase volume at lower unit cost, Ley's would also be better equipped in the future to offset the vagaries of the automotive industry by introducing some degree of diversification. Early in 1960 Ley's Foundries & Engineering attempted to buy Redler Industries of Stroud, a company of mechanical handling engineers whose products were compatible with those of Ewart Chainbelt. Although Ley's twice raised their offer for Redler, the bid was ultimately unsuccessful. Later that same year another acquisition bid was, on this occasion, successful and Ley's took over ownership of W. Shaw & Co. Ltd of Middlesbrough. This company manufactured steel castings and employed about 500 people. Their products were supplied mainly to the ship-building industry.

The updating of the Derby and North Hykeham sites continued apace during the remainder of the 1960s, the development and re-equipping of both factories following similar lines. At Derby, in 1966, a light castings unit (LCU) was commissioned in response to an increase in demand for castings up to 20 lbs in weight, thus complimenting the range of work already being produced in the 1950 Mechanised Foundry. Two four-ton induction furnaces were installed, having a melting rate of 30 cwt each. The supply of metal from these furnaces to the LCU was increased to 4 tons per hour when, a couple of years later, these furnaces were supplied with molten iron from the new 1968 melting plant.

Reference to the 1968 melting plant brings into the story the last, and probably the most ambitious, major new foundry to be built by Ley's. Planning for the 1968 Foundry began in earnest late in 1967 which, coincidentally, was at a time when the demand for automotive castings was beginning to show signs of tailing off. The output from Ley's for that year was approximately 34,500 tons, which was a figure more reminiscent of performance during the early 1950s. Only two years earlier, in 1965, the annual output had topped the 50,000 tons mark and it is interesting to note that 66 percent of the output was still in 'blackheart' malleable. The reduction in tonnage was, at the time, regarded as a hiccup in the industry, and planning for the 1968 Foundry went ahead with confidence and optimism.

The new foundry comprised two moulding lines, one being fully automatic (No.4 Line) while the other (No.5 Line) was based on the mechanisation system used in the 1958 foundry but with a casting cooling method more sympathetic to thin wall products. Utilising the buildings previously occupied by the 1926 and 'Z' foundries and constructing new buildings to accommodate new melting and sand plants, Ley's set themselves a very tight schedule to have the the new foundry operational by the end of 1968. Such was the magnitude, complexity and pressing time-scale of this project, that it warranted the use of critical path analysis (CPA) to assist in

The annealing shop, with batch ovens in the background, in 1928 in comparison to the annealing shop in the 1960s, with continuous gas/electric ovens.

The grinding shop in 1928 and below a grinding shop of the 1960s.

The moulding shop as it was in the 1920s, compared with the 1958 Foundry.

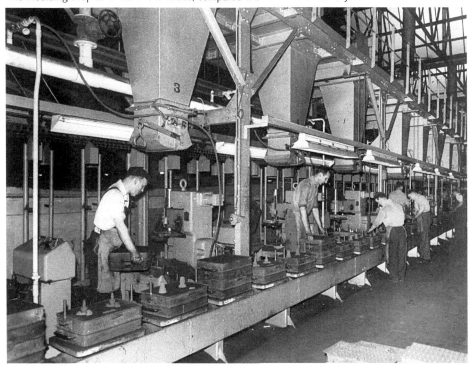

the control of planning, design and installation activities. This was prior to the installation of Ley's own computer and several years before the appearance of the micro-processor, so computer time was purchased from Loughborough University. This was the first occasion on which CPA was used by the project management team at Ley's so the valuable help from the staff at Loughborough was gladly received and much appreciated. As indicated earlier, the time-scale for the project to be up and running by the end of 1968 was extremely ambitious, and a great deal of pressure was brought to bear on plant suppliers and civil contractors to meet programme targets. Despite this pressure, delays were experienced, first due to inclement weather affecting civil work, and secondly by the manufacturer of a fully automatic moulding machine seriously under-estimating its design and manufacturing times by the substantial period of five months.

Commissioning of No.5 Line began in early December 1968 and limited production started up towards the end of January 1969, some eight weeks behind the forecasted completion date. Nevertheless, to have planned, installed and commissioned a foundry and sand plant of that nature within that period of time was no mean accomplishment. It was achieved entirely under the management of Ley's own engineering staff. No.4 Line eventually came into being in April 1969, so completing what was to be Ley's final and most expensive foundry project. More projects in core-making and processing were undertaken over the ensuing years, but by 1969 Ley's had completed all major foundry reorganisation at Derby and had utilised the site to its full capacity for mainstream products.

It now remained for the process shops to be upgraded and modernised to accept the anticipated tonnage arising from the fully mechanised foundries. In 1969 the old 'Z' end grinding and shot-blasting departments were totally reorganised. They were re-equipped with new constant peripheral speed grinding machines and shot-blast units of various types and sizes, all of which were designed to handle a throughput of 750 tons of castings per week. During the early part of 1970, an additional annealing furnace was installed having a weekly throughput of 315 tons, and at the time was the largest of its type in Europe. Very much a local affair, it was designed and installed by Salem Brosius (England) of Milford near Belper.

It was in 1969 that a name from Ley's early days was to be unexpectedly

The coreshop in 1928 and in the 1960s.

revived. The company received a letter from Mr Michael Aitken, the grand-son of H.M. Gray, who, it will be remembered, was Sir Francis Ley's right-hand man and works director during the first couple of decades of the company's existence. Henry Gray will also be remembered for his contribution to the chain business and for a particular range of chain links that were marketed bearing his name ('Gray' Chain Belt). Mr Aitken expressed a wish to set up a fund in memory of his grandfather, and he made a gift of £1,000 to enable young technicians engaged at Ley's to travel abroad for the purpose of enlarging their technical experience. The capital and interest was to be used for a period of 10 years, and so 'the Gray Travel Fund' was set up in memory of a man who played a very important role in the establishment of Ley's and, unfortunately, about whom little has emerged during research of the early years of Ley's. There is no doubt that Henry Gray played a vital role during those early years, demonstrating his abilities in most aspects of the business. Apart from his widespread responsibilities as works director, the design of a range of drive, roller and elevator chains can be ascribed to his engineering skills, but not least of all he must have carried a considerable burden during the sometimes lengthy periods when Francis Ley was incapacitated through illness.

Annual manufacturing performance throughout the first half of the 1970s averaged almost 40,000 tons, but it was becoming increasingly more difficult to maintain consistency against a background of disruptions caused by worsening labour relations in some of the major sectors of British industry. This affected Ley's from two directions, the first being difficulties with the supply of raw materials, and secondly through the dependency on an automotive industry that was experiencing frequent industrial disputes. The fluctuating fortunes of the domestic automotive market were partially offset by the company's efforts to sell castings abroad. Substantial amounts of castings were by this time being exported, Scandinavia and the US being two significant areas of trade. Another interesting and significant move away from the automotive industry around this time was the manufacture of the Pandrol casting for the railways. The Pandrol was a component part of the modernisation of track laying methods adopted by British Rail. Weighing only a few pounds each, the Pandrols were supplied as individual castings to the rail track supplier who then cast them integrally with the concrete sleeper

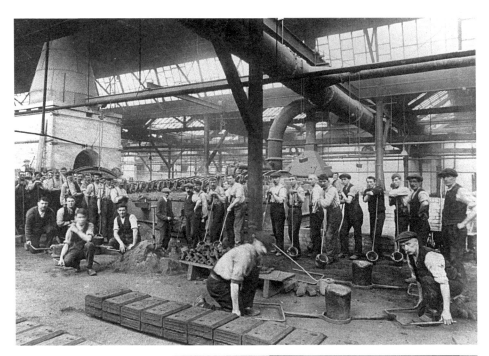

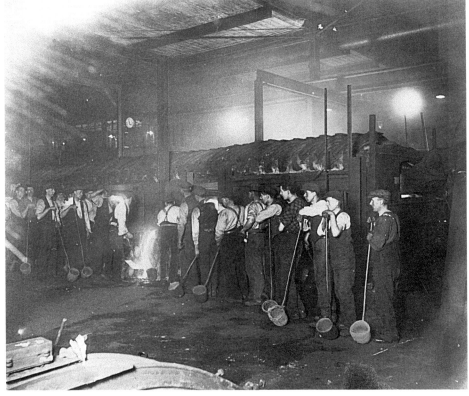

Casting in 1928 (p.138) compared with the processes in the 1960s.

to form anchors for the rail holding-down clips. For such a seemingly mundane application a high level of accuracy was demanded of this casting which involved Ley's in the introduction of a number of new manufacturing methods including automatic grinding and production milling.

It was in 1973 that the first words of warning were uttered by the board of directors. They predicted a worsening of the trading situation for 1974 due mainly to unreliability in the supply of raw materials. In the event, the annual tonnage for 1974 turned out to be only slightly down on the previous year, but with little foreseeable change in the industrial climate, the board did not see any reason to change its pessimistic view for the following trading year.

Bearing in mind the events of the past 100 years at Ley's and the company's proclivity to mark special occasions in its history, it is perhaps surprising that 1974, the centenary year, was not the highlight that many expected. Some events were organised to celebrate the centenary but, compared to other significant milestone events in the company's past, it was rather low-key. On the face of it, there appeared to be no particular reason for this, but in all probability there was a growing recognition that times had changed and the comfortable relationship which had existed between Ley's and its employees had also changed. The former bond of trust and loyalty that had prevailed hitherto was now much diluted. This situation, of course, was not exclusive to Ley's as throughout British industry labour relations were on the slide towards an all-time low, none being more conspicuous than in the industrial sectors that Ley's were so reliant upon for its raw materials and sales.

Between 1974 and 1976, Ley's experienced an improved level of trading stability which was largely due to an increase in exports of castings together with a good performance from Ewart's in its overseas markets, both of which helped to iron out the fluctuations of the home market. Ley's were now exporting upwards of 200 tons of castings per week. This was a significant factor in Ley's Foundries & Engineering being able to register a record profit for 1976 of £3.1 million, almost £1 million up on the previous year. However, once again the immediate future did not bode well, and early in 1977 Ley's started to feel the effect of a lengthy strike at the tractor maker Massey Ferguson, one of their main customers. Other automotive manufacturers were also being disrupted by industrial disputes, all of which led to an unavoidable decision in February of that year for the Derby and North Hykeham foundries to go on to a four day working week.

Notwithstanding the adverse operating conditions of this period, Ley's had not lost its appetite for diversification. In January 1977, it was announced that Ley's Foundries & Engineering had taken over the ailing Beeston Boiler Company for the sum of £575,000. This company had ceased trading at the end of 1976 with the loss of about 300 jobs and was about to go into receivership. As soon as the deal was finalised, Ley's immediately put some of its most experienced senior personnel into Beeston, and a skeleton staff of ex-employees was given the task of preparing the factory for re-opening. The incentive for regenerating the company was its strong brand image and long standing position of heating equipment supplier to many local authorities, together with an order book containing a backlog of domestic and export orders. By the second week in February the factory was back in production with a workforce of around 140, and very soon re-established itself as a preferred supplier of new and replacement heating equipment for public buildings. This brought relief to many local government authorities who had not been relishing the prospect of incurring additional expenditure had they been forced to change the supplier of their heating equipment.

1978 was a difficult trading year, with little apparent improvement in labour relations throughout British industry. There remained problems with the supply of raw materials such as coke, power supplies were becoming unreliable and the motor manufacturers were still unable to produce a consistent performance. Also, by this time, a much more sinister threat to the motor industry had emerged and was beginning to take effect – this being the ever increasing amount of imported vehicles being sold on the British market. Hitherto, the British motor industry had enjoyed a receptive market both at home and overseas, but with mounting problems of industrial unrest, doubtful quality, unreliable deliveries and spiralling manufacturing costs, their traditional markets had become tempting targets for the European and Japanese motor manufacturers. The British motoring public had become more discerning and generally responded favourably to being presented with a wider range of choice and, in many instances, a better package value. All these factors conspired to erode Ley's once reliable core business, and as the company progressed into the late 1970s this situation was reflected in the fluctuating financial picture, with a loss of £530,000 for the half year up to March 1979. At the end of the 1979 financial year it was revealed that the rate of loss-making had been reduced, leaving a final deficit of £160,047.

It is appropriate at this time to look once again at the issue of diversification, for it was during 1979 that Ley's entered into a joint venture agreement with the firm of George Fischer of Switzerland. As a worldwide engineering company, George Fischer had a number of foundries in Europe turning out products similar to those at Ley's, but their main foundry in the UK, located at Bedford, specialised in cast pipe fittings. Eventually, Ley's relinquished their financial interest in the joint venture and George Fischer took over the entire business of the North Hykeham works. Over the next few years, Ley's entered into two further business deals, another joint venture with S.&A. Malleable of Johannesburg, South Africa and a part ownership of Aranzabal of Bilbao, Spain.

The following year, 1980, saw a slight improvement in stability in the British motor industry and with Ley's continuing policies of improving export sales and pursuing diversification, this financial year produced a pre-tax profit of £1.17 million. This result, however, did not give rise to lasting optimism as, before the figures were released during the following February, the tide had turned yet again. Ley's were again compelled to introduce short time working owing to a drop in demand for its castings. Numerous redundancies had to be made and once more the company found itself in a loss-making mode.

CHAPTER 6

1981 to 1988

IN FEBRUARY 1981, Sir Francis Ley, having succeeded to the baronetcy a
year earlier, announced his decision to retire during the following month.
He had been with the firm for 53 years and had held the position of group
chairman since the death of his father in 1944.

Looking back over the career of Sir Francis, there can be no doubt that his
commitment to the company and its employees was total. He will be clearly
remembered by Ley's employees as a dedicated leader who was deeply
devoted to the advancement of the company and to the welfare and well-
being of its workers. He was always approachable and, during his regular
tours of inspection through the works, employees felt able to voice opinions,
suggestions and even complaints. Without fail, he would treat all such
comments with fairness and with whatever level of gravity they deserved.
One thing was certain, the heads of departments would very soon learn of
them. He also possessed a very acute sense of cost control and personally
viewed all departmental costs on a monthly basis. Any adverse movement in
manufacturing costs would immediately attract his attention and
departmental heads were expected to be able to provide a reasonable and
accurate answer for such occurrences. Such was the depth of his involvement
in company and public affairs, it is fitting that a closer and more detailed
view is taken of just a few of the activities in which he was involved and
towards which he dedicated so much of his time and energy.

Taking firstly a snapshot of his public life, it was in 1939, at the age of 32, that he first became a magistrate. Ten years later he took up the position of chairman of Derby County Magistrates Bench and for many years served as a Justice of the Peace.

In a lighter vein and as a prominent Derbyshire public figure, in 1952 he was asked to perform one of the county's most famous and traditional duties – that of throwing up the ball at the Ashbourne Shrovetide football game. This he did on the second day of play, the first day's throwing up of the ball having been performed by the Duke of Devonshire. On this particular occasion, the game ended all square after the two days of play with score of Up'ards 1 –Down'ards 1.

Sir Francis had a great enthusiasm for field sports and countryside matters and was associated with the Meynell Hunt and the Ashbourne Shire Horse Society, the latter body making him their president in 1954.

In October 1954, on behalf of Ley's Malleable Castings, he presented a pair of solid silver candelabra to the County Borough of Derby. These were received on behalf of the Borough by the Mayor of Derby, Alec Ling, and took their place among the civic treasures and other gifts received from Derby firms to commemorate the granting of charters to Derby by King Henry II and Queen Mary. A year later, he was listed among the nominations for High Sheriff of Derbyshire and in the following year, 1956, took up the office. This was followed in 1957 by appointment to the office of Deputy Lieutenant of Derbyshire.

He was also a leading figure within societies connected to the ironfounding industry. At various times he held high office in the Council of Iron-foundry Associations, the National Association of Malleable Ironfounders, the Worshipful Company of Founders, the Institute of British Foundrymen and was also a Freeman of the City of London.

1957 was the year in which he and Lady Ley celebrated their silver wedding. To mark the occasion a dinner was held in Ley's messroom. This event was held over two nights with about 500 employees attending on each evening. Sir Francis and Lady Ley were presented with an oil painting and a Crown Derby coffee set by Mr J.W. Fisher, a senior moulder at the foundry. During his speech, expressing thanks for the gifts, Mr Ley made reference to the silver wedding gifts given to his grandfather and father in 1913 and 1924 respectively, adding that they were still in his possession and being well cared for. Yet another example of the special relationship that had prevailed over the years. He also announced that the sum of £68,000 had been allocated for profit sharing to be paid the following Christmas. At the time this share-out was equivalent to two weeks wages for each qualifying employee.

A similar event was held at the North Hykeham works when Sir Francis and Lady Ley were presented with a radiogram by the works manager Mr G.A.R. Wildsmith. In addition to long service awards, this event was also marked by a gift of £100 from Ley's to North Hykeham's new church hall appeal fund.

1957 was indeed a busy year for Sir Francis. He attended yet another ceremony, this time in Chalfont St Peter, Buckinghamshire. Here he performed the opening ceremony for a new club house at the Chalfont Epileptic Colony. The new club house was named Ley House in memory of his grandfather, Sir Francis, and was made possible through the generosity of Alison Boyd-Carpenter, the granddaughter of the first Sir Francis and daughter of Ethel Boyd-Carpenter, the younger daughter from his first marriage to Georgina. Many years earlier, Ethel Boyd-Carpenter had been awarded an MBE for her work with the Epileptic Colony.

In 1961 another MBE was bestowed upon the Ley family, on this occasion it was awarded to Sir Francis for the services he had rendered while the holder of various public offices over a period spanning two decades.

It is hoped that by high-lighting just a few of the activities and organisations with which he was associated, an appreciation will be generated as to the amount of time he devoted to matters beyond his day to day responsibilities for the business.

In matters concerning the welfare of Ley's employees, Sir Francis could always be relied upon to take a personal interest. For many years schemes had been in existence for the well-being of employees who found themselves in unfortunate circumstances, such as long-term illness, but from time to time cases of hardship arose that did not fall within the guidelines of such schemes. In these instances Sir Francis would take a particular interest and deserving cases would not go unheard or unresolved.

He was an ever-present figure at the annual long service awards, always held with dinner and entertainment in the Colombo Street messroom. This event was one of the highlights of Ley's social calendar and was widely regarded as a gratifying feature of employment at Ley's. Two of these ceremonies which took place during the 1950s are worth recounting. The first occurred in February 1951, when Sir Francis was presented with a gold wristwatch and illuminated address on completion of 21 years service. He then made presentations to more than 60 employees. Earlier in the evening during the speech making, a number of interesting statistics were revealed when it was stated that, since inception of the long service scheme, 1,049 employees had received awards for 21 years, and 172 for more than 40 years. The speaker went on to claim that these figures could not be equalled by any other firm in Derby or, it was believed, by any other firm in the country. Another speaker, responding on behalf of the workforce, dealt with the good relationship between workers and management and stated that the Francis Ley Memorial Fund had, up till then, provided convalescent holidays for 532 workpeople and their families. It was also pointed out during this speech that workers at Ley's had enjoyed the benefit of holidays with pay long before any national agreement was agreed with trade unions.

The second long service awards ceremony of note occurred the following year in January 1952, when the record attainment of 30,000 tons of castings manufactured during 1951 was celebrated. The 1952 ceremony was the first presentation dinner attended by Ian Ley who, at the age of 17, was about to complete his final terms at Eton before beginning his National Service. His presence that night was especially memorable for the large illuminated sign constructed by Ley's electrical department staff bearing the message: '*Welcome to the 4th Generation*'.

It is hoped that this brief look back at some of the events in the career of Sir Francis will go some way towards making known the broad width of his commercial and public endeavours and the high esteem in which he was held in both fields.

In retirement, Sir Francis continued to pursue his love of field sports, maintaining his support of the Meynell Hunt and taking every opportunity to enjoy his shooting and fishing. Having sold Shirley House in 1980 to a member of the Thornton (chocolates) family, he took up residence at Pond House in Shirley where he remained until his death in May 1995 at the age of 88.

Sir Ian F. Ley (1934–)

Shortly before the retirement of Sir Francis, the board of directors had invited Ian Ley, who at the time was deputy chairman, to succeed his father as group chairman. Now at the age of 47, Ian Ley had already served 26 years at the firm so was well qualified to assume the responsibilities now required of him.

His career at Ley's had started in 1952 soon after he completed his education at Eton. Three months were spent at the foundry before he reported to Carlisle to begin his National Service with the 10th Royal Hussars, with the advantage of having gained some military experience beforehand as a member of Eton's Cadet Force. On completion of training, he attained the rank of 2nd Lieutenant and for a period served in Germany as a commander in Centurion tanks. Towards the end of his National Service, while stationed at Salisbury, he was involved in a motor accident at Virginia Water in Surrey from which he sustained serious injuries. The accident occurred in June 1954, but happily he made a full recovery in time for his demobilisation later that year. Back in civilian life, he continued his military involvement by joining the Derbyshire Yeomanry with the rank of full lieutenant.

On his return to the business, he began a systematic tour of experience and familiarisation through all the departments. He also undertook the usual trip to the US to study the latest foundry equipment and production methods, also taking time to maintain business and personal links first set up by his great-grandfather.

The Derby works long service awards for 1955 were held over two evening events in October of that year, and the occasion was also used to mark the 21st birthday of Sir Ian which had occurred on 12 June. He was presented with a silver tankard on each of the two succeeding evenings on behalf of the employees of Ley's and Ewart's. The following month, a similar event took place at North Hykeham where Sir Ian was presented with a cartridge bag and 400 cartridges by Mr Harry Hayden, the works manager.

Sir Ian was married to Caroline Errington, daughter of Major and Mrs G.H. Errington MC of Monkton Farm, Figtree, Southern Rhodesia (now Zimbabwe), on 29 July 1957, the ceremony taking place at St Michael's Church, Chester Square, London. Lady Ley had received her education in Pretoria, South Africa and later went on to spend time in France and Austria studying languages. Her father, Major Errington, had been awarded his

Fauld Hall near Tutbury, the current home of Sir Ian and Lady Ley.

Military Cross at the battle of El Alamein in 1942 while serving with the 10 Hussars. On completion of his army career he emigrated to Southern Rhodesia in 1950 to take up cattle ranching.

The following November, Sir Ian and Lady Ley were present at the 1957 long service awards dinners held over two evenings at the usual venue of Ley's messroom. The event also celebrated their wedding and in the customary manner the employees had responded to the occasion and presented the couple with wedding gifts of a canteen of Royal Crown Derby cutlery and a refrigerator. An interesting feature on one of the evenings was that a seat of honour was reserved at the top table for Miss Alice Keeton, who at the age of 80 was the firm's oldest employee. For almost 73 years she had worked as a cleaner. Starting work in 1884 at the age of seven, she had helped her mother to serve coffee to the workmen arriving at the foundry before 6am. Soon after, she was taken on to the payroll but in addition to her early morning duties she also returned to the firm in the evenings to clean the offices after the staff had departed. During the evening's celebrations she was asked by a local reporter whether she had been entertaining thoughts of retirement, her reply was, '*Why?*' She held the unique distinction of having served the firm under all four generations of the Ley family.

Another Ley's institution Sir Ian was introduced to during 1957 was the works staff outing Christmas dinner. This event was, for many years, held at the Osmaston Park Hotel until, in 1959, the venue was changed in favour of the Derbyshire Yeoman. It was always recognised as an occasion when everyones reputation, regardless of their position within the company, was laid open to good humoured ridicule. Sir Ian was not immune to this irreverence and, to mark his first appearance at the dinner, a short poem was published in the programme of proceedings for the evening. Under the title of *A Christmas Thought*, it went as follows:

Tonight is a fitting occasion
To welcome the fourth generation
First Francis, then Gordon, then Francis again
Next 'twill be Ian holding the rein.

For eighty odd years we have weathered the storm
Making castings of quality which to pattern conform
To you Mr Ian, may we suggest
Copy your forbears and we'll do the rest.

After their marriage, Sir Ian and Lady Ley lived for a short time at Shirley House before moving to Ednaston, and finally from there to their present residence, Fauld Hall near Tutbury in Sir Ian's ancestral Staffordshire. Fauld Hall, built in the mid 17th century, with additions made in the 18th and 19th centuries, is situated on elevated ground about ¼ mile south of the River Dove. The mention of Fauld will immediately bring to mind the explosion that occurred there in November 1944. Reckoned to be the largest single explosion of World War Two to have occurred on UK soil, it took place in the disused gypsum mines which were occupied at that time by the RAF as a munitions store. Fauld Hall, lying to the north-east of the centre of the explosion, suffered some structural damage to its south-west corner and to the roof and dormers. A few years ago, a thesis was produced by Virginia Thommason, the daughter of Sir Ian and Lady Ley, which deals with the history of the house in a very detailed and comprehensive manner. Virginia, born on 1 May 1960, has three children, Jack, Laurie and Cicely, and now lives in Oxfordshire. Her brother Christopher was born on 2 December 1962 and is now an Insurance Broker based in London. On 23 July 1999 he was married to Henrietta Nicholls and they have a daughter Lottie.

As an example of his many duties within the industry, Sir Ian served a three-year spell, from 1968 until 1971, as chairman of the National Associations of Malleable Ironfounders, a post previously occupied by his father between 1947 and 1955.

Sir Ian has carried forward the family tradition of service to the public and in 1985 was appointed to the office of High Sheriff of Derbyshire. This is one of the oldest offices under the Crown and one that historically carried considerable powers regarding law enforcement. Nowadays, the office of High Sheriff no longer has a direct responsibility for keeping the Queen's Peace, but the appointee is expected to develop a theme for their term of office. Sir Ian, in addition to his ceremonial duties, chose to direct his efforts towards matters concerning the Derbyshire Constabulary. Since 1983 Sir Ian has remained in touch with the foundry industry through his position as a non-executive director of Russells Foundry in Leicester.

As if the commercial problems confronting Ley's during the late 1970s and early 1980s were not enough, the forces of nature conspired against them during the first week of July 1981. A fierce summer storm broke over the Derby area producing a deluge of such volume and suddenness that most parts of the factory were flooded before any defensive action could be taken. One of the reasons why Ley's site was affected so badly was that at the time demolition of the north side of Colombo Street was taking place and, as the land drained towards Ley's from the Shaftesbury Street area, there was little remaining to slow down the surge of surface water. The main office was severely affected with the basement being flooded to a considerable depth, destroying or at least damaging some of the company's archival material. Despite the great efforts made throughout the night to rid the site of standing water, production was affected and did not get back to normal for several days. This event occurred at a time when labour relations at Ley's had taken a turn for the worse. Since the end of June, some departments had been operating an overtime ban and had also tabled a claim for increased pay on the basis of increased workloads. With production being at a standstill due to the flooding, the entire workforce were given time off and the factory gates were closed. This was interpreted as a lock-out by some union representatives, who claimed that management were using the flood as an excuse to shut down the plant to save money. For the first time in its history, Ley's experienced workers massed at the main gates in direct conflict with management.

Very little seemed to be going right for Ley's. Demand for their products had declined, foreign competition was biting hard, labour relations had soured and its capital reserves were haemorrhaging at an alarming rate. The half year results up to the end of March of that year had revealed a loss of £1.6 million. Clearly, a situation had developed which could not be allowed to continue for very much longer.

Such events were not confined to Ley's but reflected conditions that prevailed in many sectors of British industry, and in particular those associated with the automotive industry. However, in Ley's case, a major contributory factor, that was unavoidable in the manufacture of malleable iron castings, was the high cost of energy, and when this was combined with significant reductions in throughput the overall production costs very quickly became disproportionate and unsustainable.

For the next 12 months, Ley's management made every effort to turn the situation around, but the odds were very much against success. The commercial climate was unfavourable, and an increase in sales could not be generated in a domestic automotive industry that was not only reeling from the pressure of foreign competition but was also undergoing radical changes in its technological and manufacturing philosophy. Two aspects of this, for example, that struck at the very core of Ley's livelihood, were the move towards front wheel drive vehicles and an increase in the use of lighter materials.

Attempts to cut costs were continually being made through further reductions of the workforce and the imposing of strict limits on spending. In September 1982, the company played one of its final cards – it appealed to the entire workforce to forgo its claim for higher pay and, instead, to take a 10 percent cut in wages and salaries. To say the least, this proposal from management was not received with too much enthusiasm and a protracted series of meetings followed in an attempt to reach a negotiated settlement.

Before any wage settlement could be reached, and less than two months later on 4 November 1982, the board of directors of Ley's Foundries & Engineering, together with the board of W. Williams & Sons (Holdings) plc announced that they had agreed terms whereby Williams were to make recommended offers for all the ordinary and preference shares in Ley's Foundries & Engineering plc. This announcement brought to an end 108 years of direct association with the Ley family. The feeling among the workforce was generally one of mixed emotions. Those remaining, after several rounds of redundancies, comprised mainly people with long service to the company and who had witnessed the agonising decline of the previous few years. As such, the 4 November announcement was an emotional jolt. Most employees had realised that some form of essential change to the business would eventually have to be made, but this did not lessen the impact of the change of ownership and the mixed emotions of regret and apprehension and hope for the future that went with it.

For Williams, the acquisition of loss-making Ley's Foundries & Engineering was a major coup. After beating Tarmac in the take-over battle, the purchase price agreed was £3.1 million, yet Ley's had no borrowings and had assets valued at £10.5 million. This, their first major acquisition, provided the springboard from which Williams built up a worldwide conglomerate comprising many well known leading brand names spread across a variety of industries.

Soon after the takeover at Ley's, it became apparent that a significant slimming exercise was required in both plant and personnel in order to reduce manufacturing costs and to restructure the company to bring it into line with the current demand for its products. This required a large-scale reorganisation of the site which, ironically, due to the way in which it had evolved to increase output, made it relatively easy to reverse the procedure. Systematically, the Colombo Street end of the foundry was run down and key operations and service departments were transferred to the 1968 end of the site. Abandonment of the 1958 process shops presented an opportunity for Ewarts to vacate some of their old, inadequate Victorian buildings adjacent to Osmaston Road and move into the more up-to-date ex-Ley's buildings. On completion of the first phase of the reorganisation of Ley's, demolition of much of the Colombo Street end commenced. Within the space of a few months, the 1958 foundry, 1961 office block, core shop, water tower and the 1950 Mechanised Foundry were among the buildings to be demolished. While this was going on, plans were being drawn up to section the vacated site into eight separate sites for the development of small industrial units.

Meanwhile, other plans were being devised to change some of the remaining production units and finance was made available for the replacement of equipment deemed unsuitable, either by reason of high running costs or ranges of castings no longer commercially viable. While this reorganisation was in progress, the workforce of 600 received the news that approximately half their number were to be made redundant. The announcement was made on Friday 9 March 1984 and the scale of the cutback took many by surprise, as the evidence of investment in reorganisation had given the impression that business was improving and confidence growing. Other measures taken alongside this reduction of the workforce were the change from two to single shift working and the cessation of high volume SG casting production.

A few months later, the future of Ley's was again threatened, this time by striking South Wales miners who, by their action, had seriously affected the coke supplies on which Ley's depended for their melting operations. The problem was eventually overcome, but the demand for castings was not materialising as had been anticipated and subsequently profitability remained marginal and insufficient.

Yet again, cost cutting was high on the agenda, and one of the more bizarre methods employed during the winter of 1984–5 was the issue of thermal underwear to the entire workforce in order to enable management to reduce heating in the factory buildings. This novel experiment in cutting heating costs throughout the factory met with the co-operation of the workforce, and it was claimed by management that it would reduce fuel costs by up to £100,000 over the course of the winter.

By the end of 1985, the re-structuring was almost complete and had included the transfer of boiler casting production from Beeston to Derby on to a new plant built on the former site of the Light Castings Unit.

Ley's was by now a part of Williams Foundry Division, which comprised a number of companies with an annual turnover of nearly £17 million and employing a labour force of 800. Of this, Ley's contributed almost £8 million with a workforce of around 350. This latter figure was not to remain in place for very long, for in September 1986 more job losses were announced. On this occasion, the cause was reported to be firstly Vauxhall Motors, whose intention it was to cease manufacture of medium and heavy trucks in the UK, and secondly Austin Rover, who had experienced a major downturn in demand for their vehicles. This translated into a loss of 270 jobs at Ley's, leaving less than 100 personnel to carry on producing castings mainly for Beeston Boilers and the commercial vehicle market.

By this time, those who remained at Ley's were under no illusions as to the eventual outcome for themselves and the company. They did not have long to wait as, at the beginning of December, Williams sold a number of its companies to a newly formed holding company based in London and trading under the name of Haleworth Holdings. Ley's were part of this sale but under this new ownership there appeared to be no policy for recovery of the business and it, therefore, came as no surprise that on 1 April 1987 the depleted workforce were informed that all production would cease in two days time.

Subsequently, on 3 April 1987 after 113 years of production, Ley's was closed down, bringing to an end a company which, at one period in its history, had been the largest of its kind in Europe. It had been created by a man of drive and vision who had recognised a business opportunity and exploited it to the full. Under the custodianship of three further generations of the founder's family, the company had prospered, but, under commercial and social circumstances that developed over the last two decades of its existence which were largely beyond its control, it was finally forced to submit to these irrevocable influences.

Over those 113 years, Ley's had provided employment for many thousands of Derby people, and those who had governed the company throughout that time had never lost sight of the need and benefits of good relationships between themselves and their workforce. There are many facets to the culture that prevailed at Ley's, a number of them intangible and thus difficult to define, but suffice it to say that whatever lay behind the development of that culture it took both management and workers to generate and foster it over most of the life of the company.

The last to go in 1987. From left to right:
Mr Hambleton, Lol Oakley, Brian Storey,
Ken Muir, Peter Lowe and Ian Bembridge.

There remains just one more fact to record in the fading of Ley's from Derby's industrial landscape. That came in the form of a small, almost insignificant, notice which appeared in the *Derby Evening Telegraph* on 22 December 1988 when it was announced that the company was to be voluntarily wound up.

IN MEMORY OF THE EMPLOYEES OF LEY'S MALLEABLE CASTINGS CO. LTD WHO FELL IN THE GREAT WAR 1914 – 1918

BAXTER, ERNEST
BRAMHALL, CHARLES HENRY
BRAMHAM, JOSEPH ERNEST
BROWN, JOHN H.
BULL, GEORGE HENRY
BUNTING, NORMAN
COCKAYNE, ARTHUR
COLE, LAWRENCE
CORNER, GEORGE
CROSBIE, CHARLES WILLIAM
DORRINGTON, WILLIAM H.
FARMER, GEORGE
FISHER, LEONARD
GALE, GEORGE EDWIN
GIBBS, ERNEST
GLOVER, JOHN
GRIFFITHS, JAMES
HALLAS, LEONARD
HEAP, SAMUEL THOMAS
HICKLIN, WILLIAM

JOHNSON, FRANK
LEVERS, JOHN
LITTLER, HERBERT A.
MILNES, JOSEPH WILLIAM
PARRY, WILLIAM ARTHUR
PEARSON, WILLIAM
PICKERING, ALBERT
POYSER, ALBERT
REDFERN, HENRY
ROBINSON, FRANK
ROBINSON, WILLIAM
STEEPLES, GEORGE
STOPPARD, ARTHUR JAMES
STORER, WALTER
STUBBINGS, LLEWELYN
TAFT, WILLIAM THOMAS
VALE, JOHN
WAITE, LESLIE
WILSON, FRED
WRIGHT, CHARLES

LET THOSE WHO COME AFTER SEE TO IT THAT THEIR NAMES BE NOT FORGOTTEN.

ND - #0339 - 270225 - C0 - 240/179/10 - PB - 9781780911915 - Gloss Lamination